The Better Way

The Better Way

The Church of Agape *in Emerging Corinth*

RON CLARK

RESOURCE *Publications* · Eugene, Oregon

THE BETTER WAY
The Church of *Agape* in Emerging Corinth

Copyright © 2010 Ron Clark. All rights reserved. Except for brief quotations in critical publications or reviews, no part of this book may be reproduced in any manner without prior written permission from the publisher. Write: Permissions, Wipf and Stock Publishers, 199 W. 8th Ave., Suite 3, Eugene, OR 97401.

Resource Publications
An Imprint of Wipf and Stock Publishers
199 W. 8th Ave., Suite 3
Eugene, OR 97401
www.wipfandstock.com

ISBN 13: 978-1-60608-225-6

Manufactured in the U.S.A.

All Biblical quotes are my translation. All Hebrew texts are taken from *Biblia Hebraica Stuttgartensia*. All Greek texts are taken from *Novum Testamentum Graece*.

Contents

Acknowledgements vii
Definition of Terms Used ix
Introduction xi

1. Power Run Amuck 1
2. Power to the Powerless 26
3. Sexual and Social Power 41
4. Shared Sexual Power 65
5. Empowering Others 82
6. Empowering the Oppressed 99
7. Spiritual Power 114
8. Resurrection Power: Life Sucks, or Does It? 132
9. Relieving Others 141
10. Revisiting Corinth 157

Bibliography 163

Acknowledgments

THIS BOOK IS AN attempt to view Paul's letter to the Corinthians as a church planter, abuse advocate, and student of ancient culture living in a Post-Christian world. I have decided to adopt the image of the power struggle that existed in ancient Corinth between the dominant Roman Empire and the emerging Greek culture. I chose empire, realm, and *oikoumenē* to represent the kingdoms and world views that were fighting for power during the first century. Using empire also reflects the political implications that Christianity portrayed in preaching that Jesus was Lord, king/emperor, and Savior.

My years of ministry to people in oppression have not only challenged me to rethink the vision of the church, they have challenged me to reread the book of 1 Corinthians as a letter to both people in oppression and those guilty of oppressing others. I admit, as a middle class white male, to having privilege in both my life and view of the world. Even more, I now admit to having my theological views colored by this privilege. Paul's letter to the Corinthians is a letter to me, and those who are like me. It has also been a journey for me as well. I've never been to Corinth, but I've seen its culture. I will forever be changed through this emotional trip to the ancient city. Even though we may be guilty of oppressing others out of ignorance, Paul challenges us in love. He guides us to leave the temporary realm of fear, power, and abuse so that we may enter the stable world of love and self sacrifice for others. Paul not only guides us to this, he models this by his life, ministry, and relationships with others. 1 Corinthians is a letter of hope for the oppressed and the oppressor. It is a letter that shows us the better way of *agapē*.

I wish to thank my wonderful wife Lori for supporting me in this ministry. When we had the opportunity to leave a comfortable ministry in an established church, to plant a new church, she was not only supportive, she was enthusiastic. She has always been my best friend and partner in ministry. Her wisdom and courage inspire me to step out on faith and take risks with her in the empire of Jesus. I am also excited that she will have a ministry with or without me for years to come. My love and appreciation also extend to my three sons Nathan, Hunter, and Caleb. They have accompanied me in some of the darkest areas of Portland and yet, seem to have a joy for what we do. Even more they trust me and look to me as a model of Christian manhood. This is humbling. Whatever they choose to do in their life, I pray that they will never forget the excitement of living by faith in a fading empire.

I appreciate so much the spirit and heart of those in the Agape Church of Christ. The staff, members, and friends have not only challenged me to be a better leader, but have helped me to see the empire of God in new and exciting ways. Thanks also go to KC Hanson and James Stock of Wipf and Stock Publishing. You have consistently supported me in writing and publishing material that stretches me to learn and grow. You have also been patient with me as I try to balance ministry with writing. Thanks to Christian Amondson and Tina Campbell Owens for your patience with me in the typesetting process. I have received valuable insight and comments from Dr. Rick Oster and Dr. Kent Yinger. I respect both men and their criticisms, comments, and support in the preparation of this manuscript.

Ron Clark
Agape Church of Christ
www.agapecoc.com

Definition of Terms Used

A SHORT LIST OF terms used in this book has been comprised below. I have tried to use both traditional terms and newer translated terms so that the reader can understand my emphasis, as well as Paul's application in both our emerging cultures.

- *BCE* and *CE*—Before the Common Era and Common Era. These are now the common terms that replace BC (Before Christ) and AD (After [Christ's] Death) that have dominated our chronological scale.
- *God, gods*—I capitalize the one God (also named Yahweh) and leave "gods" for the classical mythological deities present in the ancient world.
- *Agapē*—this is the Greek word for love that the early Christians used to emphasize God's love as opposed to sexual love and friendship. I will write the word in an easier form *agape* throughout the book.
- *Caesar*—title for the Roman rulers/kings/emperors.
- *Isthmian Games*—Greek sporting events second only to the Olympic Games, which were held every two years. They alternated with the Roman's addition to Corinth of the *Caesarean Games*, in honor of the Roman king Caesar.
- *Caesar Temple* or *Worship*—The worship of Rome, the emperor, or things associated with them.
- *Empire*—I chose this term instead of kingdom to enhance Jesus' contrast to the Roman government.
- *Realm, oikoumenē, system, empire*—these are used interchangeably to suggest the reality or view of life that those in the world adopt.
- *Wannabees*—people who are not elite but want to be part of this group, even at the expense of sacrificing themselves to go where they cannot financially afford to go.

Heterai and *prostitutes*—The *Heterai* were "call girls" or "escorts" who accompanied wealthy men and were sexually solicited by them. The prostitutes were sexually exploited by the men.

Gynaikonomoi—"Fashion police," or women who made sure Roman women dressed modestly and within the honor codes of the culture.

Patronage—A relationship where an individual (client) becomes indebted to a wealthy person (patron) and repays this debt through service, moral support, or work.

Encomium—Writing in praise of a person, virtue, quality that an individual posseses.

Agora—The marketplace and gathering place of the city.

Introduction

Corinth Emerging

HISTORY OF CORINTH PART DEUX

The Beauty of Corinth

CORINTH WAS A POWERFUL city in its heyday. The early Corinthians claimed that the city was founded by Corinth, the son of Zeus, although few actually believed this in later years.[1] In ancient times the city was known for its wealth and beauty. Because of this it became a target for thieves, armies, and other powerful countries. Corinth produced beautiful terra cotta objects and Corinthian bronze, a pinkish colored metal used for mirrors, vases, and other decorative items. Many people in the ancient world developed a lust for this treasure.[2] Situated in the southern region of Greece it lay near an isthmus (land bridge) connecting two harbors; the Lechaion (at the Gulf of Corinth) and the Cenchrea (at the Saronic Gulf). Both harbors were named after the two sons of Poseidon, the god of the sea. Sailors would travel from Italy down the Gulf of Corinth to deliver supplies. After unloading their cargo they would sail south of the southern tip of Greece, called the Cape of Malea. This dangerous trip was necessary to continue trade between Italy and Asia. The common saying of the sailors was, "When you circle Cape Maleae, say goodbye to your home!"[3]

---

1. Pausanias, *Description of Greece*, 2.1.1.
2. O'Connor, *St. Paul's Corinth*, 76.
3. This is a loose translation of Strabo, *Geography*, 8.6.20.

Periander, Corinth's king in 627–587 BCE, decided to help Corinth by connecting the two ports with a paved road, nine to twelve feet wide, called the *diolkos*. The isthmus at its narrowest point was about three and one half miles wide. The *diolkos* had a wooden platform at one of the harbors. When a ship would enter the harbor it was lifted out of the water and placed on the platform. The wheels of the platform fit into grooves, four to five feet apart, along the paved road. The ship was then pulled across the isthmus to the next port. Some ships were too heavy for the *diolkos* and instead, unloaded their cargo which was then transported to a different ship on the other coast. While this involved a tremendous amount of work it allowed sailors the opportunity to travel through Corinth safely and spend time in the surrounding cities. Periander's brilliant project opened the Corinthian door to the world. Merchants, sailors, and travelers came to this city and helped it expand. Corinth was also able to charge taxes on the transport of this merchandise.

As a port city ancient Greek Corinth carried the reputation of being corrupt and immoral. While evidence suggests that this was an exaggeration, Corinth was known for prostitution. Stories suggest that the Temple of Aphrodite (the goddess of love) was filled with prostitutes who attracted men from throughout the world. These men squandered their money hence the famous proverb, "Not for every man is the voyage to Corinth."[4] The term for prostitute, sexually immoral individual, and solicitor of prostitutes was also associated with the word for *Korinth*.[5] On the Acrocorinth (a mountain high above the city) the temple of Aphrodite, opened its doors as the prostitutes descended below to the city to work and provide money for their goddess. These prostitutes truly were missional!

Other historians claim that Corinthian men were portrayed in plays as being drunk.[6] In spite of this Corinth became known for its strong war ships and cutting edge battle techniques such as the phalanx formation and heavy body armor. When Philip of Macedon, Alexander the Great's father, gained power over the Greek cities he placed Corinth in an alliance with Sparta and Athens. While Corinth continued to live in Athens' shadow, the city maintained its pride and power.

In order to honor Poseidon the city supported the famous Isthmian games, which were named after the isthmus and the city bordering Corinth, called Isthmia. These games were second only to the Olympic Games and were famous for running, chariot racing, poetry, acting, boxing, wrestling, and other events. Women were even participants in the Isthmian events. One father in a nearby city boasted that his three daughters had competed in these games. One won the 200 meter dash while another was a champion at racing war chariots.[7] The winners received a wilted celery or pine bough crown in honor of the gods and their heroic feats. It seems that Paul refers to this when he wrote, "Everyone competing goes through training, some receive a corruptible [withered] crown but you will receive one that is more permanent." (1 Cor 9:25) In Poseidon's temple many of the athletes had portrait statues devoted to them.[8] The Isthmian Games were a major part of Corinthian culture and even promoted a sense of unity, harmony, well being, and civic pride.

---

4. Ibid.
5. O'Connor, 56.
6. Fant and Reddish, *A Guide to Biblical Sites*, 54.
7. Ibid.
8. Ibid, 61.

A Story of Power

As time passed the Romans began to control the Greek regions. They allowed Corinth, Athens, and Sparta to continue their alliances but Corinth eventually rebelled. When Rome sent ambassadors to Corinth in 147 BCE the citizens dumped buckets of "filth" on their heads from the second story of a building.[9] This flagrant act of disrespect was the final straw and Rome responded by sending armies to teach the city a lesson in humility. As usual the Romans had the last word as Lucius Mummius led an army into Corinth in 146 BCE and leveled the city. The men were killed and the women, children, and freed-slaves sold into slavery. The Romans looted the Corinthian graves and the city of its art and other valuables. Most items were sent back to Rome where the Romans quickly became tired of this art.[10] However, Corinthian bronze vessels were still highly valued throughout the world. The temple of Apollo was left standing though most of the city was destroyed. Corinth had lost everything and was the victim of a brutal beating.

For one-hundred years the city was left empty with only a few temple priests and squatters settling in the town. The town of Sicyon, about six miles north of Corinth, managed the Isthmian Games during this time. Evidence suggests that wagon wheel ruts cover some of the famous sites in Corinth as well as the temple of Poseidon.[11] Shops and homes still existed but the squatters barely survived. In 44 BCE Julius Caesar began a building campaign and restored this Greek gem as a Roman colony. The city was built with a Roman grid plan and resettled with an equal numbers of slaves, freed slaves, and soldiers/veterans. Corinth had become the new home for those wanting to start a new life. Those squatters who survived however, were at the bottom of the social scale.[12] The Romans brought their culture, language, and system of government. Latin became the official language of Corinth for the next hundred years. Corinth was no longer Greek, it was Roman.

Springs were common in Corinth and connected many parts of the city. The city had ample fresh water for those seeking relief from the heat. The Peirene springs had become a local gathering place for the Greeks and

---

9. Strabo, 8.6.23.
10. Ibid.
11. Bookidis, "Religion in Corinth," 149; Gebhard, "Rites for Melikertes," 185.
12. O'Connor, 44.

their guests. Tradition stated that Bullerophon caught the famous winged horse, named Pegasus, with the help of the goddess Athena, while the animal was drinking at the site. The spring had become a place of healing, beauty, and community gathering for centuries. It was a major hangout for the people of the city as well as its visitors. When Rome rebuilt Corinth they chose to rebuild the Peirene Spring, however they remodeled it as a Roman site. The Roman arches were a reminder that Rome lay claim to any Greek history that the city wished to keep.[13]

The temple of Apollo survived the earlier destruction but the Romans made sure that they had their own reminders of Roman power in Corinth. A temple for Caesar still stands today across from Apollo's dwelling. The deified Julius Caesar resurrected the town and reminded all citizens that Rome gives, Rome takes away, therefore honor Rome. The Julian, and later, Octavian temple was elevated higher than the rest of the temples in the forum and *agora* (the gathering and market place of the city). Rome placed various reminders of this power throughout the *agora*. At both ends of the *agora* were temples to Roman deity, including the goddess Roma and the Roman Emperor. Along the south side of the shops was another reminder of Roman power, the Bema. The Bema was an elevated stone platform where the Roman governor would sit and pass judgment on the city. The Apostle Paul stood before the Roman official, Gallio (Acts 18:12–13), when a group of Jews in the city accused him of public disturbance. Paul may be alluding to this incident when he wrote to the Corinthians:

> We must all appear before the bema [judgment] seat of Christ so that each one gets what they deserve for the good or bad things they have done. (2 Cor 5:10)[14]

The Romans also adopted the common Greek deities as they rebuilt the city. Throughout Corinth were images such as Artemis, Dionysius, Fortuna, Poseidon, Apollo, Aphrodite, three statues to Zeus, Athena, and two images of Hermes.[15] These were important Roman deities, however, the temple to Caesar was higher than all of them. As one climbed the mountain behind the city, Acrocorinth, female deities lined the street such

---

13. Robinson, "Fountains and the Formation of Cultural Identity," 123.

14. All Biblical quotes are my translation. All Hebrew texts are taken from *Biblia Hebraica Stuttgartensia*. All Greek texts are taken from *Novum Testamentum Graece*.

15. Pausanius 2.2.6

as Hera (wife of Zeus and mother of the gods), the Egyptian Isis, Demeter, and Aphrodite. Rome permitted Corinth to keep a part of their history but only allowed its approved deities access into the heart of the city.

Roman power not only served to intimidate the people of the Greek city, it stripped them of their political rights. Greeks typically held assemblies (called *ekklēsia*—the term used for church) and were led by their elected officials. Greek leaders were skilled at dialogue, public speaking, and persuasion. Their role was to persuade the assembly to make decisions concerning politics and community issues. This was called democracy. A leader's power was displayed by skill, personal ethic, influence, and persuasion. However, Roman leaders claimed authority by the divine emperor. The city assembly only gathered to be informed of the edicts and were told to follow the new laws of the king. Instead of persuasion Roman leaders used force, authority, and coercion. The Bema at Corinth was a reminder that the city's history, freedom, and character were a thing of the past. Corinth was a Roman colony that was expected to look like Rome, act like Rome, and submit to Rome.

CORINTH EMERGES

During the next one-hundred years Corinth continued to emerge in this environment. The Greek language once again became the common language of the people and by the end of the first century CE, it was the official language of the city. The Isthmian Games continued to attract people world-wide. The temple of Asclepius, the god of healing, became an attraction for thousands who sought healing. While the temples of Demeter and Aphrodite were less powerful than before, Corinth continued to be a place of philosophy which led Diogenes to move to this city to study and teach philosophy. The inhabitants competed with each other as Corinthian boasting became a common description of their social culture.

> The elites and semi-elites there were not all "old money," but rather third-generation veterans and freed-slaves turned entrepreneurs, social climbers, and people of the local political prominence. It was a highly competitive environment, with these elites vying in business, in politics, and in claims to status. A host of inscriptions testify to the self promoting mentality of this echelon of the popu-

lation, who had many opportunities to rise along various social and political ladders.[16]

Corinthian boasting was a common characteristic of the community. Due to the high financial needs of the community the rich were constantly expected to give to support their city. To honor these individuals numerous inscriptions dotted the city in praise of their donors. Those who were beneficiaries of the rich also were expected to verbally praise their supporters. This added to the boasting of some and degrading of others. Education also provided a way to humiliate others and inflate oneself. The poetry competitions at the Isthmian games encouraged this criticism or flattery of teachers, elites, and leaders. Corinthians struggled to climb the social ladder. This led to discrimination against the "have nots" of their community.

In spite of oppression Corinth was emerging!

Life in First Century Corinth

Life in the first century CE was extremely hard. While only seven to ten per-cent of the Roman world lived in cities, those who did found it extremely stressful. Only three to five percent of people could read and write, which was reserved for the wealthy or those slaves trained to serve the wealthy. This suggests that over ninety per-cent of those at Corinth were among the lower classes. While the city was originally repopulated with an equal number of Roman veterans, freedmen, and slaves, by the mid 50's CE the rich became richer and the poor became poorer. This was a reflection of its Roman patronage since the culture neglected those without. Research on Paul's churches suggested that those in his churches lived at a subsistence level or below the poverty line.[17] As Corinth emerged, so did the tensions, struggles, class distinctions, and power.

Housing

Housing was not only expensive, it was limited. Those who owned a business worked extremely hard in the day and slept above or inside their shop. They spent seven days a week working and trying to provide for their families. Some scholars estimate that fifty per-cent of a person's

---

16. deSilva, "Let the One Who Claims Honor," 62.
17. Friesen, "Prospects for a Demography," 367.

income went to pay rent on a place to live.[18] In the city rent was so expensive that people had to live in groups to financially survive. Slaves or hired workers would sleep in the shops to protect them from thieves. The shops and sleeping quarters were extremely small (twelve feet high, deep, and wide) and sometimes had one opening (either a window or a doorway). The opening, which had either a wooden shutter or door, was left open during the day. The shop would have had a small oven or stove to heat the entire dwelling and sometimes cook food.

The majority of people lived in *insulae* (plural for *insula*) which were similar to apartments and found it even more crowded. Most upper levels were wooden and not well ventilated. There were no bathrooms and people used pots (in Missouri we called them slop-jars) which were kept on their floor or under the stairs. The poor lived near the top since it was the most dangerous place due to fire, weak structures, and storms. Corinth was also susceptible to earth quakes which made the *insulae* unsafe. People were crammed into the one room apartments which provided the neighbors with a wonderful aroma of human waste, sweat, and other odors during the hot summer months.

In the summer people spent the majority of their time outdoors. Cities had large open air markets, meeting halls, and courtyards for people to visit and enjoy the fresh air. Because of this the streets became overcrowded with wagons, carts, animals, pedestrians, and vendors. Since most of the city streets did not have gutters the rains would cause them to flood which would send people running for cover. The Roman satirist Juvenal describes an exciting trek through the streets of Rome avoiding those in the upper apartments who were dumping waste out of their windows onto the stone roads.[19] While Rome was considerably larger than Corinth, a simple trip through the town could become quite humiliating. The rich constantly complained of the noise in the city which would last throughout the day. Others traveled at night which added to the noise and helped deprive people of much needed sleep. Public toilets were open and completely public while those more private had "peep" holes cut into the walls for those who enjoyed removing all privacy from the occupants.[20] Living in the city provided plenty of stress, vulnerability, and frustration.

18. de Vos, *Church and Community Conflicts*, 110–16.
19. Juvenal, *Satires*, III.
20. de Vos, 31.

Those who were wealthy enough to afford houses still had to experience the day to day stresses of overcrowding. The front door opened onto the street which allowed the dust, mud, noise, and occasional stranger "passing by" to enter into the inner recesses of the home during the day. While the female sections, slave quarters, and bed rooms may have been located at the rear of the home for privacy, they were small and poorly ventilated. The dining room sometimes lay in full view of the street providing opportunity for outsiders to hear many discussions and become aware of the family's business.

Social Life and Status

> Those who were well-born were proud to display their nobility; those who had moved up the social ladder were keen to forget their social past, and those who could not move, tried to hide their true estate. Social prejudice was firmly established. [21]

Corinth had become a city with strong *social distinctions*. Those with money, Roman citizenship, and a noble family history were influential in the city. Originally this city was re-populated by Julius Caesar with slaves, freed-slaves, and nobles. One hundred years later Corinth, like any other city, had developed its own competitive social structure. The majority of those living in Corinth were poor, oppressed, outcasts, and slaves. Some slaves had worked and saved a *peculium* to pay for or earn their freedom from their master. These "freedmen" were still viewed as "lower class" but had the opportunity to work and earn their wealth and honor in the city. Other people who were free citizens were "wannabees." These individuals worked hard to look like the elite, talk like the elite, and have houses like the elite. They were also excluded from the "elite." They were people who barely made enough to survive and had little extra to show for it. However, they still tried to look as if they were climbing the social scale in their cities.[22]

The "elite" were very wealthy. They had to be. In order to hold public office one had to be able to fund construction projects, temples, and other civic expenses. Since Corinth was continuously rebuilding and seeking

---

21. Clarke, *Secular and Christian Leadership*, 62.

22. Wallace-Hadrill, *Houses and Society,* 25–26. Here Wallace-Hadrill suggests that many of the people climbing the social ladder in Roman culture enjoyed the illusion of wealth, power, and honor and displayed this in their homes.

the favor of the Roman Empire the city constantly sought the donations of private, wealthy individuals. Corinth was a city which had a special officer for the Isthmian Games, who was called an *agōnothete*. Their only responsibility was to make sure that the games had the financial support to continue. The *agōnothete* had the task of competing with many other projects to secure funding from those in the city who had money. Since fundraising involved banquets the wealthy were frequently invited to dinners which consisted of appeals for money. Only four to five percent of the people were in a position to give financially, therefore competition for their money would have been fierce.

The elite also used their money to secure favors and relationships. This was called "patronage." Wealthy individuals used their financial and personal influence to pay the debts of others, buy and rent land, and help people "climb the ladder to success." Because patronage was common at Corinth, the city was filled with tributes to the wealthy. Public places in the Roman world were a parade ground of statues.[23] Temples, plaques, and public inscriptions were physical reminders of this tribute. They served to offer praise those who gave gifts and encourage competition among the rich.[24] Those who were indebted to their patrons gave vocal and personal tribute to them. Loyalty and praise were expected from the hands, mouths, and hearts of those indebted to their patrons. While some patrons did this out of love for their city, others used patronage as a form of manipulation. Many times this further shamed and humiliated those without. However, it became a way of life. The majority of the city became indebted to those with clout, honor, and power. "The majority of saints in Corinthian assemblies were poor."[25]

HUMAN PRAISE AND HONOR WERE COMMON. THEY WERE ALSO EXPECTED.

Those who were elite were attributed with good morals. Terms such as good, noble, honorable, wise, and pure were reserved for the wealthy. These morals were not based on actions, they were based on status. The wealthy were assumed to be good while the poor were assumed to be wicked. Honor was based on social power and wealth, not conduct. The

---

23. Judge, *Social Distinctives*, 175.
24. Ibid., 176.
25. Friesen, 367.

inscriptions, verbal praise, and public display of honor were constant reminders to the lower class that they were slaves not only to Rome but to a system. Debt, slavery, and shame were a way of life. The majority of the city found a way to survive in this system.[26]

When Alexander the Great conquered his area of the world he used the term *oikoumenē* which meant the inhabited world. The word, however, came to mean the civilized or Roman/Greek controlled world. Alexander brought the Greek language to the region stretching approximately from Albania to Afghanistan. This made Greek the *common language* (*Koinē* Greek) in much of the world. This common language helped to unite the world through trade, communication, and intellectual knowledge. This was similar to the world-wide web which has quickly enhanced a common globalism. However, with the *oikoumenē* came a sense of isolation, loneliness, and desire for a personal salvation experience.

The culture responded to these needs through support from *communities*. Public clubs and fraternities such as associations, trade guilds, cults, and philosophy schools helped to provide community for all people. In these clubs the poor, wealthy, and slaves found opportunities to lead, serve, and establish a common social bond. These associations helped the poor, cared for the sick, and provided burial support for those unable to pay this cost. These were communities that provided a sense of belonging to all people in the city.[27]

With the spread of Greek culture came the rise of other *religions*. The cosmopolitan nature of Greek culture opened the way for Persian, Asian, and other Eastern religions. When the Romans became the new leaders of Alexander's *oikoumenē* they embraced these various religions as well. The Emperor cult (those who worshipped the current Caesar) however, provided no eternal salvation or thought of hope for the worshipper. It only glorified the Roman Empire. The Asian mystery religions provided personal salvation and a way into relationship and knowledge with the deity. These mystery religions grew because they provided a definite transition for the poor and a place of acceptance, teaching, and spiritual enlightenment. Rich and poor were all welcomed into these mystery religions which introduced the initiate to the story of the god, the secret teachings of the cult, and a transformation or initiation into the life of

26. Clarke, 23–27.
27. Harland, *Associations*, 26–28.

the worshipping community. These religions grew in the Roman world because they provided hope, knowledge, and support for the worshipper. However, they also began to lose their power and influence by the end of the first century CE.[28]

The Struggle for Power

Due to the limited amount of resources in ancient cities the rich and poor *struggled* for access to these goods. The ancient world is usually called an *agonistic* society. This means that people had to struggle (Greek word is *agōn* from which we get agony) to obtain precious commodities in their community. Honor was one of the precious commodities in this world. Only certain individuals could have honor. Some were born with it. Their parents may have been wealthy, Roman citizens, or sports heroes. This is called *ascribed honor*. Others tried to move up the social ladder by increasing wealth, buying honor, or taking it from another. In the Gospels when Jesus publicly confronted the religious leaders he received public honor while they lost it. This is called *acquired honor*. In the ancient world people were trying to take, withhold, and defend honor. Everyone struggled to become better so that they could pass their status on to the next generation.

There was not only a limited amount of honor but also financial resources, land, and food. The rich gave back to the community which was a sign of redistribution. Rather than hoarding their wealth, those with money and resources were expected to bless their neighbors. By making it available for all to enjoy they were showing others that they were willing to share and give to the less fortunate. Those who became more and more wealthy were seen by the lower classes as evil. The upper class saw this as wise, prudent, and their divine right. The rich monopolized the limited wealth of the city.

Patronage was expected in this culture. It was a means of survival. It was a way to bless others. It was a way to share with the poor. The wealthy were expected to fund building projects, pay the debts of others, and care for the poor. Those with money many times gave "favors" to those in need who were expected to return the favor through service, support, and supply until the debt was paid. Patronage worked in cultures where the poor needed the blessings and care from the rich. However, when misused it

---

28. Walbank, "Unquiet Graves," 278; Williams, "Roman Corinth," 246.

became a way to manipulate others. This caused resentment, competition, and discrimination. If you were without you were vulnerable.

Cultural anthropologists suggest that two commodities are common in all cultures—money and food. I would suggest a third; power. In the ancient world power was also a limited commodity. Power was not usually dispersed from above. It was reserved for those with honor, status, and privilege. Power was the life force in every civilization. Power was and still is necessary for life to exist. However, power was meant to be shared. This is called empowerment.

Rome controlled power. Rome hoarded power. Rome withheld power. However, Rome was only creating an illusion of power. In Corinth the temple of Caesar was elevated above all other temples, markets, and the city center. The old Corinthian structures that were rebuilt were designed as Roman structures. With arches and Roman statues these new buildings were only reminders of Corinth's Greek history but now with Roman flair. The official language was Latin, not Greek. The message was clear; Rome destroyed Corinth, Rome built Corinth, and Rome owned Corinth. Roman strength and power was the model of masculinity, religious devotion, and justice. The Corinthians were reminded daily that they were vulnerable and subservient to Rome; that they were indebted to Rome; and that they must see the world through the Roman lens. Rome went to great lengths to communicate that they were a force to be reckoned with. They also communicated that the Greek culture had passed.

> But Corinth continued to emerge. Most people spoke Greek. Many people resisted this hoarding of power, even though they may have been powerless.

HERE COMES PAUL

A different soldier came to Corinth with a different type of power. The Apostle Paul visited the city in 50–51 CE. The writer of the book of Acts, Luke, told us that Paul was in Corinth during the rule of Gallio, who was proconsul of Corinth around 50–51 CE (Acts 18). His brother was Seneca, the famous tutor of the emperor Nero. When Paul came to Corinth the city would have been preparing for the Isthmian games (held every two years). He stayed with a Jewish family (Aquila and Priscilla) who had been expelled from Rome by the emperor Claudius. During the 40's, Claudius had driven out select Jews from Rome because he felt that they had been causing turmoil in the city. Later, when they were allowed to return to Rome, Aquila and Priscilla continued their ministry to the Roman Christians (Romans 16:3). While in Corinth this couple made tents, which were important to the city. Sailors used these tents while in the city and during the Isthmian games, many travelers used them to camp near the competition site. Paul came at a time when Aquila and Priscilla would have needed help and been extremely busy. He would have been one of those who worked and slept in the shop below their apartment. Paul was not afraid to work hard during his ministry in other cities.

> In hard work and labor, in many nights of insomnia, in hunger and thirst, often without food, in cold and exposure. Apart from this, there is the daily anxiety that I have for all the churches. (2 Cor 11:27–28)

Roman writers suggest that those who worked with their hands were lower class, uneducated, undignified, and despised. Nobles spent little time with manual labor; because they were expected to hire slaves. Paul's work was extremely hard and required long hours. One can imagine Paul toiling with his host couple and sleeping on the hard floor much of his time in Corinth. As a laborer Paul would have been seen as less credible and of lower intelligence.[29] When he spoke in the synagogue (a place where Jews and Jewish converts worshipped) he was ignored and abused (Acts 18:6). He chose to take a step of faith and speak only to the Gentiles (non-Jewish). Unfortunately it would be this group of people who would despise his trade and speaking ability. However, God opened the door for his ministry to the masses. Paul also understood what it was like to be at the bottom of society.

Paul had been raised in Tarsus, a large city near Cilicia. Paul was born a Roman citizen (Acts 22:28) and therefore was raised in a family with honor, and privilege, who were part of the Jewish elite. He had some of the best Jewish education and was a rabbi, Pharisee, and important courier for the Jewish council at Jerusalem (Acts 22). Paul was a man who knew and studied the law of God, loved God, and would get an assignment done. He felt passionate about God and protecting the teachings of the Jews. The Pharisees were devoted to keeping God's law and people pure, uncompromised, and honored. He even went to the extreme of persecuting, killing, and consenting to the death of many Christians.

---

29. Jeffers, *The Greco-Roman World*, 24–25.

Then he met Jesus. On a mission trip to Damascus he was blinded by a bright light, rebuked by Jesus, and sent as a blind man to this city. He was vulnerable, humiliated, and given a vision. Jesus told him that he would suffer for the kingdom (Acts 9:16). He was baptized and never looked back. He became a preacher, teacher, and missionary for Jesus. Later God sent him to Corinth. God's sense of humor is displayed in sending a former Pharisee to a city like Corinth. Even Paul sensed this irony:

> I came to you with weakness, fear, and much trembling . . .
> (1 Cor 2:3)

Or to put it another way, "When I came here I was freaked out . . . " He spent his life avoiding the very people God sent him to love. Yet Paul was not afraid to push the envelope. When some in the Jewish community drove Paul away he lived with a Gentile (Titius Justus) who went to the synagogue as well. The leader of the synagogue, Crispus, and his family were baptized. God continued to work and told Paul that in spite of the small Jewish synagogue and the many Corinthian believers God had many people in the city (Acts 18:2, 10). Paul was not only sent to the Gentiles, these people were God's people. Paul stayed eighteen months until he traveled to Syria. Yet he left a church in Corinth with a great message. It was a church that was also emerging.

Paul the Evangelist

Paul is an interesting individual. I realized this a few years ago. I was a minister at a larger church and spent three years preaching through the Gospel of Luke. People liked the stories of Jesus, the patience, the power, and the compassion of Christ. The challenge to be like Jesus was never really a challenge but an aspiration. Jesus is the Son of God, perfect, and unreachable. Therefore the stories are there to guide us closer to him, call us to accept our imperfection, and marvel at the sinless nature of Christ. Then I preached through Acts. I finished it in a year and focused on the church's response to Jesus. Many of the stories were about Paul, since he was a major character in this book.

That is when I felt the tension from our church leaders. Acts is different. In Luke we have an excuse; we are not perfect like Jesus. In Acts we have no excuse. We are challenged to respond in faith and obedience. This many times convicts us in our Christian walk and ministry. The apostles were real men, with real doubts, and real faith who moved mountains. Paul was one of those uncompromising, fully committed, and highly intelligent missionary types who was abused for his convictions. Even Peter wavered after the resurrection but we identify with him because we too have compromised our convictions (Luke 24:37–44; Acts 10; Gal 2). However, with Paul you knew where you stood. With Paul there is a call to discipleship in Jesus. With Paul we observe a man who told John-Mark that he couldn't take a quitter with him (Acts 15:37). Paul was the one who went to court, spoke his mind, and manipulated a trial only to go to a higher court. Paul told a group of knee knocking sailors to stay in the boat or they would die. Paul was beaten, slapped, and rejected by his own people. Paul told it like it was and many times suffered for it. However, he has some of the most wonderful thoughts concerning forgiveness, patience, grace, and love. He was a man who lived what he believed. He was passionate for Jesus, people, and a vision.

Today he continues to suffer. While some dissect the words of Jesus many others try to dismiss most of the things that Paul wrote. His transition from the Jewish culture to pluralistic culture shocks us as he confronted their issues. When the Roman philosophers spoke concerning morality people take note. When Paul spoke others today scoff because he appears "judgmental," fundamental, and narrow minded. Yet, we have to admire Paul's commitment to the Gospel and ability to transfer it to other cultures.

Was Paul a radical? It seems that people view him as a wild eyed, crazy, and fanatical Christian. Maybe we feel this way because he was *physically beaten for his faith*. Since we haven't been mistreated for our convictions we must assume that Paul "pushed the envelope too far." However, missionaries in other countries and those in former communist countries can shed light on this issue. In their world persecution happened to those who were leaders in churches and who influenced their community. Persecution did not happen to those who "pushed the envelope" but those who were convenient targets. Because Paul was public he was a convenient target.

Maybe we feel that Paul was radical because *he spoke against the "sins of the city."* However, Paul, like many other philosophers of his day, wrote and spoke against societal issues because they had a responsibility to guide their group/disciples to moral transformation. Paul followed the normal educational method of guiding people to live a life that reflected the values of their community and belief system. Maybe we feel that Paul was radical because *he seems critical in his letters*. However, a comparison with other common writers of his day and a deeper reading of the letters suggests that Paul focuses more on acceptance, grace, and love in guiding the community. Unlike the philosophers who wrote diatribes and confined their instruction to letters, Paul worked with people, shared personal stories, and allowed relationships to form between himself and the congregations.[30] Paul was a people person. While we may have heard sermons where Paul is quoted in condemnation against *people*, they may reflect the preacher's theology rather than Paul's.

> Maybe we feel Paul is radical because *he challenges us in our walk with God*. He does. Maybe that is why he is a convenient author to ignore, critique, or dissect? Jesus is safe but Paul can be risky.

Paul Accepted Responsibility

In the letter to the Corinthian church Paul proved to be a teacher, patron, and apostle. First, *he accepted the authority and responsibility his position required*. He began the letter by explaining that he was called to be an Apostle of Jesus.

> Paul, called an apostle of Christ Jesus by God's will . . . (1 Cor 1:1)

Paul introduced this letter with an important phrase. He claimed to have been called by Jesus as an apostle. It was important for the author of ancient letters to identify themselves and explain why someone should listen. Paul was also one, as a missionary to the non-Jewish people, whose authority was questioned. He was the thirteenth apostle (twelve was the typical Jewish number for completeness) and had to prove that Jesus had called him. In this letter, as others, he claimed that his apostleship was from God (Rom 1:1; 2 Cor 1:1; Eph 1:1; Col 1:1) and by God's will (2 Cor 1:1; Gal 1 [sent]; Eph 1:1). Paul also reminded them that he was "called." Called (*kaleō*) is an interesting term. It suggests that someone is chosen for a task. Paul saw his leadership as this task or responsibility.

Paul not only told the church that he was called; he reminded them that they too were called. Paul's authority as a leader did not cause him to be distant from the church, it suggested that he was trying to live out the same mission that they had been given. Paul spoke as a leader who

---

30. Judge, 93.

was on a similar journey. However, even though he was farther down the road he had walked much of the way that they were called to follow. Paul was a guide or mentor rather than a ruler. In 1 Cor 4:15 he suggested that he was not a guardian or pedagogue. Pedagogues were slaves hired to protect, train, and teach youth. In many cases they used a rod or stick to beat the youth into submission. However, Paul desired to be a model of holiness for them. They were saints (1:2) and needed to continue to be holy. He was leading them in their walk with God. His encouragement to imitate his conduct (1 Cor 4:15; 11:1) was not out of arrogance, it was out of a desire to model faithfulness for them. He admitted that this was God's will. Paul's conversion experience, acceptance by the other twelve apostles, experience in preaching, and mission from the church in Antioch (in Syria) gave him a sense of authority (Acts 12:1-4). God had spoken directly to Paul but also through the leaders of the church. Paul understood that he had a responsibility and mission. Because Paul accepted this responsibility he was expected to lead the church to grow and develop for Jesus. He did not believe it was his church but he did believe that they were his people. However, he was their guide and had a role to play in their spiritual growth.

Paul acknowledged that he was one of many who were called to help them. The letter to the Corinthians was coauthored by Sosthenes. Sosthenes is also an important character. In Acts 18:17 he was in charge of the synagogue at Corinth. Synagogues were small gatherings of Jews and Gentiles, who had embraced Judaism and gathered to worship God and discuss community events. Because the temple was located at Jerusalem the Jews who were scattered throughout the world needed places to form community and gather weekly (Saturday) to hear the word of God read out loud, discuss the stories, and worship. The synagogue was also a major meeting place during the week for Jews as well as a place of teaching and prayer. When Paul came to Corinth (Acts 18) he baptized Crispus, who was in charge of the synagogue at that time. When the Roman official at Corinth, Gallio, refused to let the Jews punish Paul for preaching about Jesus, the Jews beat Sosthenes (probably Crispus' replacement). We don't know why but somehow this man decided to join Paul in his ministry. He was a co-author with Paul in a letter to his hometown. Sosthenes was a Jewish convert to Christianity who knew how to live for God in a city rejecting that God. He was also willing to suffer for Jesus and his vision.

Authority as a Team

Paul also had a mission team that accompanied him on his journeys (Acts 20:4–6). It is likely that his team helped with his messages. This suggests that Paul and Sosthenes *worked with a team to model the life God called the church to live*. In 1 Cor 3–4 Paul wrote that they were farmers, builders, and common workers. They worked hard to help the church be what God had called them to be. They were expected to model hard work, humility, faithfulness to Jesus, and a counter-cultural attitude concerning their relationship with others. Their role, as leaders, was to model a ministry that built the church. He also called himself their *father* (4:15) or *patron* indicating that the church's responsibility was to imitate his way of life.

Research on ancient letter writing suggests that Paul would have used a scribe/secretary to compose his letters.[31] Rom 16:22 indicated that Tertius wrote Paul's letter. While scribes arranged, inserted, and dictated material it was the author who bore the authority for sending the document (Gal 6:11). Paul's letters would have been written, reworked, dictated over a period of time, and suggest that Paul, and some of his team mates, would have had a collaborative effort in the production of many of the letters. One can imagine Paul, Sosthenese, the team, a scribe, and those reporting the news from Corinth (1:11) gathering together and composing, re-reading, editing, and inserting material in an effort to produce a letter to take back to the church. This suggests that Paul and his team used resources to minister to each church. I can almost see the group smiling as the scribe wrote:

> Then you will not be proud against each another... (1 Cor 4:6)

We have typically viewed Paul the letter writer as a man hunched over a desk, writing the words on paper as the Holy Spirit dictated each word to the Apostle. Others imagine Paul, under the influence of the Spirit, pacing back and forth dictating the letter to Sosthenese. In the United States we have strict rules concerning plagiarism, letter writing, and inspiration. However these rules should not be forced onto letter writing techniques in another culture over two-thousand years ago.

First, *the ancient Mediterranean world was not individualistic*. Since the invention of the printing press, Europeans and Americans have placed an emphasis on the written word and individual reading of the texts. The

---

31. Richards, *Paul and First Century Letter Writing*, 64–80.

ancient world saw inspiration, writing, and reading as a group process. The Holy Spirit works in community:

> Without guidance a nation falls, but many advisers bring victory. (Prov 11:14)
>
> A fool thinks that their way is correct but a wise person listens to advice. (Prov 12:15)
>
> Without advice plans fail, but with many advisers they succeed. (Prov 15:22)
>
> Where two or three come together in my name, I am there with them. (Matt 18:20)

Second, *because the ancient Near Eastern world believed in community inspiration they did not consider borrowing, sharing, and collaboration on a text as plagiarism.* Scribes were hired to work with the author to create, arrange, add to, and edit a document. However, the author took responsibility for the final product.

Paul the Model of Spirituality

Paul also served as a model of spirituality to this Christian community. First, he *modeled sacrifice for the benefit of the community.* In 1 Cor 9–10 Paul and the team willingly sacrificed their personal rights to help others draw closer to God. While other church leaders had the right to marry or be supported by the churches, Paul's team chose to work while at Corinth. Those in the city had the right to eat whatever they wanted but the team suggested that what was important was another person's conscience. They chose to live in order to help others, even at their own expense.

Paul modeled spirituality by *faithfully passing on the traditional teachings of Jesus and the church.* Paul wrote that he had been faithful in teaching key concepts of the Christian life. This involved the life and crucifixion of Jesus (2:2), that Jesus was the head and men and women were not independent of each other (11:2, 11), the Lord's Supper (11:23–26); and the death, burial, resurrection, and appearing of Jesus (15:3–8). For Paul the basics of the Christian life had been taught and practiced while he was in Corinth.

Paul also *applied Jesus' message to those in a different culture.* The church had questions concerning marriage (7:1–2), eating meat at local spiritual banquets (8:1–3), spirituality (12–14), and the financial collection for Paul's relief ministry (16:1–4). Throughout these chapters Paul discussed Jesus' teachings and claimed that his opinion/teaching was approved and considered authoritative by the Lord (1 Cor 14:37). Paul knew that being a leader and mentoring the church required him to speak with authority and give clear direction to the people.

Paul also *modeled a Christian lifestyle as a leader*. He suggested to them that he, and the team, had given them a model of hard work. Their willingness to be considered part of the common class of people also reflected Jesus' lifestyle and humility. In chapters 8–10 he continually held himself as a symbol by seeking the good of others and appealed to them to follow his example (11:1). In chapter 14 he reminded the church that he would gladly give his spiritual giftedness away in order to encourage others in the church (14:18). Paul's use of the word "imitation" also indicates that he had a close relationship with the Corinthian Christians.[32]

Paul knew that *some were limited in their discipleship with him, yet he provided another way*. Paul acknowledged that his practice of sexual abstinence was personally important, but not a requirement for the church (7:7). While he stressed that being single was good, living for the benefit of others was more important. If they or their spouse could not be abstinent, couples should provide for each other sexually. Families were to promote peace, sexual enjoyment, and support for each other. While some could be single they needed to be concerned about their partner's desires rather than their own.

Paul also *practiced presence* in the church. He acknowledged that he had lived among them and taught them the teachings of the faith. However, even in his absence he claimed to be present in Spirit (5:3). As a Roman colony the Corinthians knew that the emperor was present even while he was in Rome. His authority and *parousia* (presence) still reigned in his absence. A letter from the emperor to the community stressed the ruler's authority and presence as well. Paul also used phrases such as "I encourage you," "I praise you," "I remember you," "I thank God for you," and others to stress his personal relationship with the church. Paul was a leader who had relationship with the people in the church.

Paul gave them hope, even while he was gone.

---

32. Bellville, "Imitate Me," 121, 123. Judge, 151.

Agape and the Reset Button

Not only did Paul practice leadership, he expressed *agape*/love as a common theme throughout the letter. As a leader Paul would have wanted the letter to address major issues in the church. However, he did not use judgment, abuse, or a strong rebuke. Pau indicated that the Corinthians needed a place to ground their identity.

I have constantly read that the church at Corinth was a congregation full of sin. I have heard preachers talk about their churches as "like Corinth." Once when I was speaking to a group of Korean ministers I used Corinthians as a text to talk about church leadership. I was asked why I used this letter because the church was "so bad." I mentioned that we were looking at how Paul led a struggling church and encouraged me, as well as them, to lead churches struggling in our various cultures. When most people think of the letter to the Corinthians they think of controversial issues, sin, and wickedness in the church. However, the letter reflects Paul's leadership style to a people needing guidance.

> Grace and peace to you from God, our father, and Jesus Christ.
> > I always give thanks to my God concerning you, for God's grace has been given to you in Jesus Christ.
>
> That in everything you may be:
> > filled in every word
> > and all knowledge
>
> even as Christ's testimony is confirmed in you;
> > so that you do not lack any gift
> > > since you are the ones waiting for the revelation of our Lord Jesus Christ.
>
> He will confirm you until the end and choose you in to the day of our Lord Jesus Christ.
>
> God is faithful, who has called you into fellowship with his son Jesus Christ our Lord. (1 Cor 1:3–9)

In these first few verses Paul emphasized who they were. They were holy, chosen, spiritual, and in fellowship with God. Just as the many stone pillars and plaques in Corinth confirmed the honor of those who gave money to the great building projects in the city, so God confirmed these Christians through love and relationship. While we know that Corinth had a troubled church they were similar to churches today. Paul had a good relationship with them and could confront them. But—he appealed to their new nature in Jesus.

My boys are good at video games. When I was their age we played PONG. You may remember this as the game with two paddles and a ball. In 1976 it was the new Wii. However, playing video games (if I can still use the term video) are much more advanced than when we turned the big knob to play PONG. Now the games are much faster and interactive. When I play Wii or Nintendo 64 with my boys they usually win. There are those rare occasions that my thumbs have a mind of their own and I begin to win major battles. Then it happens. They hit the reset button. Time stops. The screen goes blank and then the word "Reset" appears. This sends me into orbit and I stand (adrenaline coursing through my veins) and say, "Are you crazy, I was winning," to which they reply, "I wasn't . . ." The reset button starts the game over. The past is gone, the defeat is avoided, and they get a fresh start. If I could hit three buttons with two fingers I would do what they did, but I can't. The reset button is valuable because it is a new starting point, a new game, and a chance to even the score in the battle.

In 1 Corinthians Paul continually appealed to who they were. While addressing their behavior and struggles he designed a thread of support and identity as their *reset* button. Verses in the document served to remind them to reset the action. One can almost imagine the team suggesting that the scribe stop and insert a reset button in the document. These verses called the church back to their relationship with God. The reset button reminded them that their motivation was not fear but God's love, calling, and election.

- 1:2 They are holy and called to be holy.
- 1:4 They are spiritually complete, Jesus is with them, and strengthens them.
- 2:16 They have the mind of Jesus.
- 2:12; 12:7–13 God freely gave them the Spirit.
- 3:9, 16, 22 They are God's building, temple, and Christ's possession.
- 5:4 Jesus is present among them.
- 6:11 They have been transformed.
- 6:15, 19; 10:1; 12:27 They are member's of Jesus and God's temple.

- 7:17, 20, 22, 23 They were called and bought with a price.
- 8:6 They live in Jesus.
- 10:13 God will not abandon them.

Paul even asked them if they would rather have him come with a stick/rod (as a pedagogue) or with love and a gentle spirit. He seemed to believe that they needed guidance and support rather than force and power. Paul reminded them that they were in relationship with and possessed by God and the Spirit. These reminders were their "reset buttons." Paul seemed to weave these reminders throughout the letter to encouraged and guide them to repentance, growth, and healing.

Reset 1: Identity

There are valuable lessons in this letter for the modern church. *First, those of us who are in Jesus must consistently be reminded of who we are and who we are supposed to be.* The word "called" is similar in the Greek for chosen, invited, and singled out. God has *invited* us to be with Jesus and be in relationship. This is not a privilege, it was a gift. We are invited because God loves us. Some accept this invitation and others reject it. We, however, have chosen to respond to God's call which is to be a blessing in our lives (6:11).

We are holy and are called to stay that way. I often hear that we are all sinners. Others suggest that we are flawed. Sometimes I hear this because Rom 3:23 is misquoted to suggest that we are all sinful.

> . . . since all have sinned and fallen short of the glory they are justified by a gift of grace through the redemption of Jesus Christ . . . (Rom 3:3)

While I understand that we sin, we will sin, and we will struggle with sin—the text does not say we are sinners. It suggests that we are better than that. Rom 3:23 is not meant to be condemnation for all humans. The text was written to Christians at Rome who had been baptized and put away sin (Rom 6–7). Rom 3:23 only states that we all sinned (past tense) and are justified or made righteous (present tense). This is only through Jesus. Paul appealed to who the Christians were in Christ. Likewise, in light of all that the Corinthians had experienced Paul reminded them that they were holy—therefore they were to pursue a life that was distinct from the sinfulness of their environment (1 Cor 1:2). The Corinthian Christians were to develop and mature as a normal body should.

Agape develops spiritual maturity. *Agape* is the Greek word for unconditional love and is used in 1 Cor 13. The word also translated "perfect" (*telos*) means maturity. Perfection is unattainable but maturity is expected and attainable. *Agape* is also a fruit of spiritual maturity. In Matt 5:43–48 Jesus showed us God's maturity through *agape*.

> You have heard that you should love your neighbor and hate your enemy. I tell you to love your enemy and pray for the ones who persecute you, so that you may become sons of your father who is in heaven, who causes the sun to rise on the evil and good and the rain to fall upon the righteous and unrighteous.
>
> If you love the ones who love you what reward do you have?
>
> Don't tax collectors do this?
>
> If you greet only your brothers what more do you do than others?
>
> Don't the gentiles do this?
>
> You be mature as your father in heaven is mature. (Matt 5:43–48)

Agape causes us to mature in the eyes of God and the church. God has invited us to be holy and therefore spiritually mature. Spiritual maturity develops as we live out our calling in a community that pursues love and holiness. Jesus gives us this strength. The church, as the body of Jesus, is a place to grow. We develop locally and universally as a body of people invited to fellowship, holiness, and love. You are called to this as a person in God's image and as part of a group.

Not only do we need a reminder of who we are, we need strong leaders to guide us to maturity. This second lesson applies to leadership. *Leaders must focus on reminding others of God's love.* Paul provided a great example for Christian leaders. His style in these two letters involved building up the body by reminding them who they were called to be. Typically leaders have felt that church growth and development begins by pointing out the sins of all people, God's anger at sin, and then describing their need for Jesus. However, this says very little about God's love for people. This can be effective temporality but it doesn't last. Leaders need to understand that a high majority of people entering the faith come from dysfunctional life stages. They too are emerging out of the ashes of destruction. Those who leave addictions, self-destructive patterns, and abusive or dysfunctional families tend to enter the faith with a low view of themselves. They receive this because their family of origin may not have given them the love, support, and nurturing that they needed.

Humans are created for community. God has designed us to be dependent upon, loved, and accepted into a family or community at birth. Human babies are the most helpless in the animal kingdom because they are completely dependent. Because of this dependence we need to be "filled" with love and self esteem. When children reach adolescence, they struggle to move from self centeredness to become giving, mature adults. Maturity means giving back or sacrificing for others.

Many people, however, enter this world through a family that does not fill them with love, respect, and support. Some have been emotionally drained, abused, and/or neglected as children. Others at some point have their childhood ripped away through trauma, sickness, or addictions. These people face life as empty vessels in need of substance, love, respect, and attention. Many of the Corinthians also came from these backgrounds. Slaves, lower class outsiders, upper class citizens and elites, women, and children all needed acceptance. Leaders like Paul have to begin with this self-esteem issue when working in ministry.

Reset 2: Relationship

In the beginning of this letter Paul appealed to the Corinthian's relationship with God. Paul knew that this letter must address the sin, struggles, and issues that the Corinthian Christians faced. Paul also appealed to their relationship to God as a foundation throughout the letter. This foundation suggested that no matter what had happened, they were in relationship with Jesus.

First, Paul mentioned that this relationship *originated with God's love*. Throughout the Bible God initiated relationship. In creation God initiated order out of chaos (Gen 1; Psalm 8). After the flood God initiated relationship with humans even though "Every desire of their hearts are evil from childhood," (Gen 8:21; 9:11–17). God sent prophets to warn people so that they could repent (Ezek 3:20–21; 18:32; 33:33). After the Jewish people were taken captive to a foreign land God initiated a new covenant (Jer 16:14; 31:33–34) In 1 Cor 1:18–24 Paul wrote that God had initiated their relationship by calling/inviting them. God had chosen the weak in Corinth. The Christians needed to know that God always initiates relationship with people.

Second, a relationship with God *involved blessings*. In 1 Cor 1:1–9 Paul used the word that is translated "call" four times. The term for church means those *called* out to hear the message of God (1:2). Paul mentioned that they were *called* holy (saints) with others who were *called* throughout the world (1:2). In 1:9 Paul wrote that they were *called* into fellowship with Jesus. God *called* them out from a world of sin, gave them grace, and revealed the knowledge of Jesus to these Corinthian Christians. God initiates relationship by choosing, blessing, and revealing power and love to a people lost in sin and darkness.

Reset 3: Agape/Love

Paul also weaved the theme of *agape* love throughout 1 Corinthians. The Corinthians lived under the rule of a "divine" Roman emperor. This empire claimed to provide Roman peace (*Pax Romana*), power, and presence in the cities of the empire. This empire was the new *oikoumenē* that Alexander claimed to establish. However, Paul believed that this kingdom was incomplete. He wrote that their system/empire was temporary. Their leaders, world, and time were passing away or being abolished (1:28; 2:6–8; 4:5; 7:31; 13:8). However, love (*agape*) was to be permanent (13:8). This love was mature (complete), permanent, the greatest quality, and a motivation for ministry. Throughout the letter Paul called the church to act out of love and encourage each other. This *agape* was the better way, rather than the system/empire they had accepted (that was passing away). It was the ethic of the church and one that caused them to mature and develop into completeness. The church was in tension between two empires: the way of power or the way of *agape*.

Faith development authors suggest that unconditional love is an advanced stage of spiritual growth. To practice unconditional love (*agape*) helps the Christian and faith community mature and become complete. This practice of *agape* places other's interests above one's own. It helps Christians reflect God's *agape* and encourages others to transform their lives. As a leader Paul modeled *agape* as he sacrificed, developed, and guided them to transform their lives. The Corinthian Christians were called to practice *agape* and also mature into adulthood (13:8–12). Paul's challenge to imitate his practice of *agape* gave Christians a model for spiritual development and maturity (1 Cor 4:16–17; 11:1). For Paul *agape* is the "perfect/complete" or "mature" quality of the faith. Yet it exists in tension with that which is imperfect/temporary.

I believe that the letter to the Corinthian Christians is not just a letter about a corrupt, sinful, screwed up group of people. It is an important letter about leadership. Paul, as a Christian leader, used the "reset button" often in this letter. The "spiritual reset button" was the constant appeal to their relationship in Christ. They were reminded that God initiated their relationship with Jesus and continues to do so through Paul and the other leaders. Paul suggested that *agape* could help heal, transform, and develop them to be what God wanted them to be.

I once had a minister tell me that he was probably going to be fired from his church. He said that people wanted "feel good sermons." I responded with, "Why is that bad?" He said, "When you have a whole church of hypocrites they need to be warned and told to repent."

> I wondered what reset button he used?
>
> Maybe it was a stick.
>
> I wondered if there were a few good people there.
>
> Maybe he should have tried love and a gentle spirit.
>
> Maybe he couldn't hear God say, "I have people here in this place..."

Paul suggests that the path to transformation continues when we have "spiritual reset buttons" in our lives. Guiding churches to repentance and change does not depend on spiritual beatings but reminders of:

- Who God is
- Who God wants us to be
- Who we are.
- Who we are meant to be.

In the midst of our struggle to see Jesus face to face we fall. However, we need reminders of who God is. We need to be reminded of who we are. We need appeals to who we are meant to be.

> *We* need to press the reset button.
> Sometimes *we* need *someone* to press the reset button.

Leaders and Discipleship Today

I have been a minister for over twenty years. During this time I have taught Bible/Ministry majors in undergraduate colleges and seminary. I have also spent years working with ministers and church leaders. I have met many godly men and women who daily lay their lives down for those in their congregations and communities. I have been challenged by their love, maturity, and spiritual wisdom. I smile when I think of them sitting in the scribe's office listening to Paul and the team editing the letter. I could see Paul looking to them for input and the opportunity to join in on the conversation.

However, I have met many others in ministry and school who worry me. They cause me concern about the future of the church. I am not concerned because I think that they are "doctrinally in error." I worry because of their work ethic, their lack of relationships with unchurched people, and their commitment to spiritual development. Even more I worry because some of our academic institutions and public lectureships/conferences hold up as models those who are disconnected from their local communities. They may be great speakers but they can't speak from ministry experience. Their time in the office crafting sermons is nice, but they don't speak to those in the marketplace, the streets, or even the pews. They have little presence in the congregation or the community. I also think that many of our people in churches are frustrated because they want Paul but they are told they really need an orator. Therefore, they learn to settle.

When I read Paul's description of himself in 1 Corinthians (and other letters) I see a man who had relationship with those in the community. He became all things to all people to win them (9:22). He toiled at his job in the community (4:12). He sacrificed for others in his ministry (8–10). He didn't read a book about Post-modern or Post-Christian culture, he knew the city of Corinth and tried to speak the Gospel in their language. He had a relationship with them and they trusted him. He worked in the marketplace, saw, and experienced the temptations of daily life. He also resisted them! He was not a man who retreated to his office every day—his office was in the *agora*, among the people.

1 Corinthians is not a letter about a church that was sinful. It is a letter that shows leaders what it means to disciple a congregation. It is a letter that reflects a "pastoral heart." It is a letter that comes from a man who lived among the very people who he had been raised to hate. He was willing to violate his traditional personal space to eat, sleep, and hang out with those "unclean" Gentiles. While some see Paul as a radical trouble maker, for me he is quite the opposite.

In 2006 my family and I left the traditional church structure that we had grown to love. I had preached for over twenty years in this structure but we realized that it too was passing away. In a nation that was emerging to find its own identity Christianity was seen as part of the old *oikoumenē*. A movement that once united the world had now created a longing for salvation and a feeling of isolation. Living in Portland, Oregon where statistics claim only fifteen percent of people went to church; we saw the need for churches to emerge as well. When we left to plant a new church in downtown Portland, Paul's letter to the Corinthians became much more valuable to me. Trading my office for Starbucks, an open area at Pioneer Courthouse Square, or a homeless community (Dignity Village) has taught me what it means to study and teach the Bible among the people. Studying and teaching Corinthians in these environments gave me a new appreciation for Paul's letter. This was not because we were working with "Corinthians" but because we were doing ministry alongside a culture that was emerging from the ashes, speaking its own language, and being forced to see their history through Roman arches. Power and honor were limited goods, however, people wanted to leave their agonistic society for a better way.

As a church planter who worked side by side with community service providers to help the oppressed, homeless, abused, and traumatized I quickly saw how power was hoarded rather than shared. Power was a precious commodity but it was not available to all. Even more, the church was reflecting its cultures' withholding of power. We were withdrawing from our communities. Unfortunately, my years in the *oikoumenē* style of ministry had not taught me to dispense power, only how to keep it safe. We were afraid of our church becoming another Corinth, therefore we could not say, "and such were some of you . . ." Yet our fear kept us from eating in the home of Titius Justus (Acts 18:7). It was time for me to emerge as well and become a leader who could guide people, practice the presence, and speak the Gospel in a culture with a different language. It was also time for me to mature by practicing *agape* with my community which wanted to know more about Jesus.

THE BETTER WAY FOR AN EMERGING CULTURE

We live in a world that is similar to the *oikoumenē*. It does to us what it did to those in the early centuries of the Roman Empire. It creates loneliness, a desire for community, and a longing for salvation. It drives us to lust for power, only to feel powerless. It causes spirituality to fade and become lifeless. However we return to the spiritual because we long to be spiritually whole. In some ways English has become our world language, yet this is not what drives the *oikoumenē*. It is not the world-wide web, globalism, media, or commercialism. While these are powerful forces in our system they do not drive the *oikoumenē*.

Power

Power has always driven the *oikoumenē* and will continue to drive this empire. We are united globally by power and we are isolated because of it. We rise out of the ashes through power and we fall below because of it. We live with power and die in spite of it. Power drives the *oikoumenē*.

- Human trafficking is the number one money making industry in the world today. The weak are sold for money, a limited good in the *oikoumenē*. The weak are sexually exploited for people to pursue happiness in the *oikoumenē*. Male privilege uses this power to exploit others.
- Drugs, guns, and pornography have now dropped below human trafficking in the *oikoumenē*, but still occupy a place of power. These are also power players in the market of limited goods. Again, male privilege uses this power for self gratification.
- $450 billion is spent by Americans at Christmas. $10 billion would solve the world's water crisis.
- The United States is one of the three worst countries in the United Nation's world system for children. Children suffer in the land of the free and home of the brave.
- One in three women world-wide admit to being physically abused in their lifetime.
- One in six men has admitted to being sexually molested as a child.
- Three million children yearly witness a traumatic event in their lives.
- Racism still holds a position of acceptance in the *oikoumenē*.
- Genocide still strikes fear in the hearts of people worldwide.

- Caring for the poor, oppressed, and marginalized in our communities are no longer a defining characteristic of Christianity. They have become an option.

Rick McKinley, Sr. Minister at Imago Dei Community Church in Portland, once stated, "We should worship God, love people, and use things. . ." In the *oikoumenē* this is reversed.

In spite of this the institution of unlimited power, the Christian Church, is declining in modern day Rome (United States). The seat of power is no longer the empire of God. We no longer have a voice worth hearing. Yet in the *oikoumenē* something is emerging. Something is rising out of the ashes. Something finds a way to survive in the midst of power. Something emerges in spite of what Rome says. Something acknowledges that this limited good exists only in this *oikoumenē*, not the empire of God.

Paul saw an emerging community and knew that they needed guidance. Paul the stiff necked missionary became the gentle shepherd of a community struggling to find a way to exist in the *oikoumenē*. While many have expressed that the church at Corinth was a wicked church, a group of foul mouthed sailors needing forgiveness, or sinful people run amuck; I see them as products of the empire of power. They, like many of us, lived what they knew. They walked where they were led. They returned to what they had been taught.

Paul knew that they needed a reset button. Like so many today, those in the *oikoumenē* need time to regroup. We have lived in a world of power that has abused us for so long that it seems natural, to us, to be defeated, discouraged, and oppressed. When the empire of power regularly kicks your butt you have no option but to bend over, ask for more, and take it with a smile.

"Thank you sir, may I please have another?"

You find a way to survive. You live in the world of power and limited good. You compete in the agonistic society and watch your honor and status slip away. However the empire of God has its own reset button.

The reset button reminds people that they are in God's image. One day I was taking one of my trips downtown to find a young person spanging (begging) on the street and take them to lunch. This was a common practice of mine and one that helped to attract visitors to Agape. I rode the light rail train downtown while reading *On the Resurrection* by a second century Christian writer named Athenagorus. Athenagorus was an ancient Eastern Greek Christian. Eastern Christian writers tended to focus on the resurrection, community, and seeing God more clearly. This was different from Western writers who focused on the cross, our sin, and the individual. According to Athenagorus Jesus came because our world was so dark that we could not see the Father. Because of Jesus we had a clearer view of God. His goal was not to remind us of our sin but to open our eyes to the glory of God. I was reading this and listening to Bon Jovi's *Have a Nice Day* when I came to a kid flying a sign. He was asking for money to eat and wrote that he smoked pot for Jesus.

We had a nice lunch and talked about how the preachers in the courthouse square preached that people were going to hell. He just wanted to smoke pot to experience Jesus. I told him what Athenagorus said (and maybe a little of what Bon Jovi sang). I let him know that Jesus wanted to remove the crap from his eyes to see God. We talked about his past, his family, and how he was treated and I knew why he couldn't clearly see God. However, I reaffirmed what Athenagorus claimed that humans were worth saving, were in God's image, and that he was deeply loved by God.

I don't know what happened to him. I do know that I have had many similar conversations with other youth and I see them at church more and more. I do know that he, like many others, lives in the *oikoumenē* and is trying to find a way to survive. However, standing at the square, condemning people, and going back to the suburbs was not the way of Paul. Calling people to repentance, working among them, guiding them, and offering them love instead of a rod was and is a better way. The reset button is not sin or guilt. It is and will always be the *agape* of God and the church.

I have seen this *agape* work. "Love Portland" is a massive project driven by some of the city's emerging churches. During the summer many of us give unconditionally to our communities by rebuilding, painting, cleaning, and donating supplies. Public schools are cleaned, homeless camps are rebuilt, shelters are painted, the hungry are fed, and parks are cleaned. Thousands of people come together to work for our city. The first openly gay mayor in Portland has praised the churches for this work. We at Agape call our weekend (during this time) *Agape Blitz*. We have worked side by side with the homeless, Reed College students (one of the most liberal colleges in the US), other college students, city officials, and those who resent our church worshipping in their public school. Homeless people from our church clean a school in the richest neighborhood in Portland, and CEO's help turn a tent into a walled structure. What drives all this is *agape*. What brings glory to God is *agape*. What draws people back to the churches is *agape*. *Agape* drives the empire of Jesus. *Agape* is truly the better way.

When Paul asked the Corinthian church to imitate him it was because he practiced *agape*. Paul gave them the tool to mature and heal their divisions. He gave them the power to empower others. Paul called them to a new *oikoumenē*, a new kingdom, and a lasting empire. He showed them how to have healthy marriages and treat the opposite sex with respect. He challenged them to change how they saw themselves, how they saw others, and how they saw their world. He reminded them that the *oikoumenē*/empire of Rome was temporary but something else was permanent. He showed them who they were and why God loved them.

He showed them *agape*.
He shows us *agape*.

1

Power Run Amuck

1 Cor 1:10–17

I encourage you, brothers and sisters, on account of the name of our Lord Jesus Christ that you all come to an agreement; that there is no division among you; and that you might be knit together in agreement with the same purpose. Those from Chloe's family have reported to me, my brothers and sisters, that you have personal alliances. Each of you says:

I am Paul's
or I am Apollos'
or I am Cephas'
or I am Christ's

Is Christ divided?
Was Paul crucified for you?
Were you baptized in Paul's name?

I am thankful I did not baptize anyone but Crispus and Gaius, so that no one can say they were baptized in my name (I baptized Stephanus' family but I don't think I baptized any other). Christ did not send me to baptize but to preach the good news—not with wise words so that the cross of Christ become useless.

IN THIS SECTION PAUL mentioned that he had heard a report from Chloe's household/family. The Greek word for household and family (*oikos*) is essentially the same word. In the ancient world family comprised everyone in the same dwelling. This included parents, children, grandparents, widowed members, divorced members, slaves, business associates, and homeless or aliens to a city. Chloe was most likely a wealthy woman (either a widow or Christian married to an unbeliever) who sent her slaves/messengers to inform Paul of issues in the church. In 16:17 Paul mentioned that Stephanus, Fortunatus, and Achaicus arrived and delivered something to him. The last two names were common slave names and it is likely that they are the messengers sent from Chloe. Since travel was expensive it is possible that Chloe or Stephanus were able to fund this trip.

These informants have told Paul that the church was struggling with various issues such as:

- Quarrels/division (1:10)
- Sexual sin (5:1)
- Lawsuits among members (6:1)
- Marriage and sexual relationships (7:1)
- Food/meat given as a sacrifice to idols (8:1)
- Eating as a family in church (11:18)
- Spiritual gifts (12:1)
- The resurrection (15)
- The collection for Paul's relief efforts (16)

In 7:1 Paul mentioned that a letter had been written to him which may have concerned these issues. Probably Chloe's messengers carried this written correspondence to Paul and the team for input concerning certain issues. 1 Corinthians seems to be Paul's response. Paul desired to help the church address these problems. In 1 Cor 4:14–17 Paul seems to summarize this section by explaining why he wrote the letter. This issue, which Paul addresses, comprises approximately one-fourth of the letter.

Paul began this letter by addressing a major problem in the congregation. According to Chloe's messengers there was conflict in the church, which caused division, quarrels, and suggested that they were forming allegiances to Christian leaders such as Apollos, Paul, Cephas (another name for Peter), and Jesus. Paul wanted them to quit fighting and work together.

He asked them to be united in speech, knowledge, and understanding. This translates to having the same attitude and purpose in the congregation.[1]

What was the root of this problem at Corinth? Division! These Christians were forming allegiances to some of the leaders. Apollos was a Jewish man who knew the Scriptures and the way of Jesus well. Paul's friends Priscilla and Aquilla met Apollos while they were in Ephesus (where Paul had left them—Acts 18:24–19:1). Apollos only knew John the Baptist's baptism (baptism with a view to the coming of Jesus—see Acts 19:1–6) but Priscilla and Aquilla taught him Jesus' way more accurately. He later went to Corinth (Acts 18:27–19:1) to teach. Somehow while he was there a group of people (maybe those he led to Christ) formed a loyalty to him. Others formed loyalties to Paul, who may have first taught them. Some formed a loyalty to Peter (Cephas is Peter's name in another language called Aramaic). Still others claimed a loyalty to Jesus. It is possible that the Corinthian Christians met in different homes for worship. The patrons of these homes may have hosted Paul, Peter, or Apollos while they were there. These men or women would have felt a connection to their spiritual leaders and may have felt that their house church needed to support the Christian leader that they connected with.

Greek people were very heavily influenced by teachers, leaders, and influential people. In ancient Greek and Roman culture, one's loyalty to a teacher was not only seen in support (financial and verbal) of that teacher—it was also displayed by an ability to criticize other teachers. Dio Chrysostom was a historian in the first century who visited Corinth. He wrote about a visit to the temple of Poseidon where he found the community competing with each other for honor.[2]

> That was the time, too, when one could hear crowds of wretched sophists around Poseidon's temple shouting and reviling one another, and their disciples, as they were called, fighting with one another, many writers reading aloud their stupid works, many poets reciting their poems while others applauded them, many jugglers showing their tricks, many fortune-tellers interpreting fortunes, lawyers innumerable perverting judgment, and peddlers not a few peddling whatever they happened to have . . . The crowd that gathered was composed of strangers, and each of these, after speaking or listening for a short time, went his way, fearing his

---

1. Howard, *Paul, the Community, and Progressive Sanctification*, 149.
2. Dio Chrysostom, *Oratio* 7.9.

refutation of their views. Just for that reason, said Diogenes, he was like the Laconian dogs; there were plenty of men to pat them and play with them when they were shown at the popular gatherings, but no one was willing to buy any because he did not know how to deal with them.

Powerful people who lived in a empire of power contributed to these divisions. Many of these people demanded loyalty and devotion from their disciples, clients, slaves, or subjects. Some of the terms he used for divisions, factions, and strife were used by Greek and Roman historians concerning the political conflicts between the Greek city states and the Roman government.[3] Paul felt that the empire of God was not supportive of oppression but empowerment. Paul's method was not control, but the guidance of the Spirit (2:4–5). In the church there was no need to control or exploit others. In the church there was no need for the people to feel afraid of or intimidated by their leaders. Leadership was not about loyalty, it was about empowerment. Leadership modeled *agape*.

Wisdom was also a valuable and powerful quality in the ancient world. Ancient historians suggest that three to five per-cent of the population could read and write. In a large Roman city, such as Corinth, the percentage may have been higher. Some of these elite would have been slaves who were trained to serve in the government. These slaves would have had a higher status due to their education. In the ancient world, knowledge brought power and honor. Knowledge was also a commodity to be preserved rather than distributed. Education was for the elite. It provided power over people as well as power to help people.

This concept was reinforced by some of the Mystery Religions in the ancient world. Mystery Religions began in Asia and were later embraced by the Greeks and Romans. These were secret groups that claimed to have special knowledge and insight into the worship of a god/goddess. Mystery also meant *initiation* where the person choosing to enter that faith went through instruction, a rite of passage, participation in a play/story, and sometimes baptism. This produced a loyalty to the deity, the group, and the leaders. The individual was to keep the truths of this faith secret (hence the term Mystery Religions) and be devoted to the group. A mural on a wall at Pompei shows the scenes of the Dionysian Mystery. The final scene has the initiate viewing themselves in a mirror. The dim reflection illustrated their transformation into a new world of knowledge and power.[4]

3. Welborn, "Discord in Corinth," 143–44.
4. Nappo, *Pompei: A Guide to the Ancient City*, 154–57.

Mystery Religions were not the only groups promoting loyalty and initiation. Schools of philosophy required this loyalty and devotion through initiation. Many of the Jewish sects such as the Dead Sea Scrolls community, Pharisees, and Sadducees also became "schools" where followers went through initiations and stayed loyal to the leaders. In the Jewish *Mishnah* and Talmud (traditions of the Rabbis) schools formed around influential leaders, teachers, and scholars. Devotion to a leader and quoting the scholars helped to promote the truth and value of one's conviction and therefore helped to gain them new converts. This continued even after the death of the teacher.

In the Roman Empire this was a form of *patronage*. A wealthy individual (*patron*) would pay the debts of others (*clients*) with the expectation of praise, adoration, and service from them. The patron might teach or mentor an individual who would be indebted to them for life. The patron could humiliate, encourage, or even abuse these clients until they had paid their debt in full or indefinitely depending on the relationship. A Roman comedian, Juvenal, tells a humorous story of being a *client* who was invited to dinner at his *patron*'s house.[5] These clients were confined to a separate room, from the wealthy guests, and given the worst food imaginable. Juvenal ended with the statement that, he had paid his debt in full after this meal. The abuse of inferiors, while not supported by Roman etiquette, was practiced often.

This practice continued in the church. New Christians, especially those of the lower classes, would have felt a sense of loyalty toward their teachers or spiritual patrons. Their loyalties to their patron and criticism of other teachers/patrons would have created an environment of divisiveness and rivalry. For Paul the issue was clear. His use of words for jealousy and strife reflect the typical competitiveness of Corinthian culture.[6] The church involves teamwork, empowerment, and love. Jesus is the true patron and the teachers worked as a team to build up the church. Greeks valued harmony and the church needed to not only uphold this value of society, it needed to reflect Jesus' unity in the body.[7] The actions of the members did not give credibility to Paul, Apollos, Jesus, or Peter. Paul

---

5. Juvenal, V.

6. Judge suggests that jealousy (*zealotes*) was a term to follow a teacher by creating strife (*eris*). See Judge, 179, Winter, *After Paul Left Corinth*, 36–37; and Clarke, *First Century Christians*, 179.

7. de Vos, 36; deSilva, 61–74.

reminded them that their salvation was not dependant on their teachers, but on their own faith; and that their divisiveness presented a threat to their salvation (3:10–17). The body (church—not individual bodies) is a dwelling place for God's Spirit. To destroy or divide the church was to attack the Spirit and God. While this was the way of the *oikoumenē*, Paul warned them that divisiveness was not the way of the Spirit or *agape*.

Jesus as Patron

Paul introduced his argument by challenging the church. First, *he suggested that Jesus brought unity* (1 Cor 1:10, 13). Jesus came to unite people rather than divide them. The divisions were human centered—not Christ centered. The Christians were using human alliances in the church to praise some and manipulate others. They were mixing their worldly governments, educational systems, and business relationships with the empire of God. For Paul, the church and the way of *agape* involved loyalty to *Jesus* and unity and harmony with each other.

Second, *divisiveness happens when we believe that our calling or being chosen makes us better than others*. We fail to acknowledge that we were chosen, not because of who we are—but because of who God is. As Paul reminds us, God chose the lowly to shame/humiliate the proud. Our election is by grace. God chose to love us. Therefore we should extend that same grace and love to others. God/Jesus is our true patron and if we wish to boast, it should be about him (1:31).

Finally, divisiveness hides our feelings of inferiority. The endless giving to receive praise or self worth only makes us empty. It is a giving that comes from our own insecurity. Therefore, we need affirmation because we are not affirmed in who we are. We are not able to set boundaries, we are not able to say "no," we are not able to take a break and care for ourselves. This causes divisions because we become enablers and care-takers. We, in turn, do not empower others. We cannot love others because we do not love ourselves. The way of *agape* applies to us as well.

While current research suggests that the church is declining in North America, the church still holds a sense of power in our communities. I have never been persecuted as a minister or a Christian. Most of the time people show me a tremendous amount of respect. Lori and I have freedom to go most places which are off limits to regular people. As a couple in ministry we receive trust, support, respect, and power from many people in our community. The church, even today, holds a sense of power in the lives of people and the community. Ministers too hold this same sense of power, respect, and honor.

When a minister has a sexual affair with a member of the community, they abuse their power. When a church leader mishandles money they abuse their power. When a leader uses their position to hurt, manipulate, or coerce others, they abuse their power. When a leader has to have control over a church they abuse their power. When a minority of people in a church refuse to compromise or yield "their choice" they create divisions. This is contrary to the empire of Jesus because the power of the Spirit and *agape* empowers others. *Agape* does not assume that "I am right," but believes that God can work in a group of believers. The church and leaders are called to help people draw closer to Jesus. They are to help people be the best they can. They are to promote unity in the church, not deception and fighting. They are people of peace and love, which manifest the power of God. They are people who use their knowledge and wisdom to help others grow. Knowledge, power, and relationships are dispensed rather than withheld.

The church today can learn from Paul how to empower others. Christianity in the US has become more inward focused and has begun to alienate itself from our society. We pull our kids out of the world to protect them. We have stopped going into our community and instead retreat from it. We do not develop healthy relationships with people who do not know God. Because of this our churches have begun to complain because we have lost the respect and influence we once had (at least the influence we thought we had). Yet, Paul tells us in this letter that our calling is to empower people, encourage people, and help others develop their relationships with God, who works in and through us to empower others to bring glory to Jesus.

For church leaders, we are less concerned with holding correct doctrine than we are with empowering people to discover Jesus. Leaders are not measured by how much they know, but in how they effectively move people in their walk with Jesus. They are measured by their ability to love unconditionally. This involves spiritual wisdom and maturity. This provides a different type of experience and faith. This faith and Godly wisdom believe that God can transform lives, beginning with us. Leaders should let God guide their ministry in the way of *agape*.

THE HUMILIATION OF CHRISTIANITY

Paul next discussed Jesus' crucifixion and its meaning in the church. Crucifixion was both torture and public humiliation. If you were lucky, you died quickly. The entire process of crucifixion involved humiliation through a trial, physical beatings by whips that contained fragments of bone, metal, or rock, public taunting, and carrying your own cross through winding streets. Victims of this torture usually defecated and urinated on themselves, bled profusely, and would have vomited. Next they were hung by their arms and feet (which were nailed to the wooden cross). The slow process of suffocation, exposure, and continued public disgrace not only destroyed the victim's life, it broke their spirit. If they did not die quickly their legs were broken with a large wooden pole which would hasten their suffocation. Pain and humiliation were constant companions throughout this entire process.

The process was so brutal that a Roman citizen was exempt from this punishment. It was not right to humiliate a Roman citizen but everyone else was fair game.

> Jesus died this shameful death. God once again was humiliated by the ones created in the divine image.

The message of Christianity began with
- Shame
- Humiliation
- Suffering

> All chosen and experienced by Jesus.

Paul tells us that Christianity began in Corinth with the oppressed, the outcasts, and the dishonorable.

> All chosen by God.

1 COR 1:18–31

> The message of the cross/crucifixion on the one hand is stupid to those being destroyed, but it is the power of God to those healing.
> It has been written:

> I will destroy the wisdom of the wise and frustrate the understanding of the intelligent.

Where is the wise one?

Where is the scribe/professor?

Where is the visionary of this realm?

God has made the wisdom of this world stupid.

Because of God's wisdom the world did not know this wisdom.

Since Jews ask for signs and Greeks seek wisdom—it seemed good to God, through the "stupidity" of preaching, to save those who believe

> Therefore we preach the crucifixion of Christ which is an offense to the Jews and "stupidity" to the Gentiles.

> However, Christ is the power and wisdom of God for those of us who are called (Jews or Greeks).

> God's "stupidity" is wiser than that of humans.

> God's "weakness" is stronger than that of humans.

Consider your calling, brothers and sisters:
not may were wise according to human standards
not many were powerful,
not many were noble

>> but God chose the stupid things, according to this world, to shame the wise
>> and God chose the weak things of this world to shame the strong
>> and God chose the dishonorable of the world and rejected and things that are
>>> nothing to cause the things that are "something" to pass away.

So that no one can boast before God.

Because of him you are in Christ Jesus who has become our wisdom from God
righteousness
holiness
redemption

As it says, "Let the one who boasts boast in the Lord."

In the Greek and Roman world wisdom was a prized possession. Musonius Rufus was a popular Roman philosopher during the time of Paul. He felt that wisdom united men and women.[8] Wisdom and phi-

---

8. Winter, *Roman Wives*, 59–61.

losophy brought salvation to people. To know and understand meant that one had a path out of themselves. Most major religions suggested that knowledge was a means to bettering one's life.

Wisdom also was a goddess (Sophia—which is the Greek word for wisdom). She was divine. In Egypt, Mesopotamia, and Canaan the god's revealed wisdom to the chosen ones who dispensed this wisdom to others. Wisdom brought order in a chaotic world. Those who hoarded or withheld wisdom had tremendous power in their communities. They had power!

Paul also mentioned that the Jews wanted a sign. During his time the Jews were looking for signs that the kingdom of God was present. They were living under Roman rule, aliens in their land, and a nation scattered throughout the world. The Jews looked to Jerusalem to be the city that reflected the glory of God and unite all Jews scattered across the face of the Roman world. The prophet Isaiah promised that Jerusalem would be a place to draw outsiders close to God:

> Arise, shine, for your light has come, and the glory of *Yahweh* has risen upon you. Look, darkness shall cover the earth, and thick darkness the people; but *Yahweh* will rise upon you, and the glory will be seen over you. Nations/Gentiles will come to your light, and kings to the brightness of your rising. (Is 60:1–3)

For Paul, God gave power and wisdom to help those who were called and chosen. First, God's wisdom (because it empowers the weak) lay outside of the "world's" wisdom or the *oikoumenē* (1:21, 25). It existed in an empire vastly different than the temporary empire of Rome. Even though the Jewish scriptures taught that wisdom empowered the weak, their leaders had accepted the current view of the world. They, like everyone else, tried to use power to oppress others and keep outsiders out. Jesus consistently confronted the Jewish leaders who took advantage of the poor, oppressed, and sick. This was never the way of God or the way of *agape*. However it was a common issue throughout history. People in power many times misuse that power. For Paul, this was not the way of Jesus or the way of *agape*.

God's wisdom and power changed the way that the culture viewed the world and its people (1:28). God's wisdom has always challenged those abusing power. God sent prophets, priests, messengers, and the Son Jesus to call those in power to act out of compassion, love, and justice. God chose men and women from various backgrounds to stand and deliver the words of justice and righteousness. They confronted the oppressors and supported the righteous. Those who cared for the poor and needy were modeling the heart and ministry of God. Many of Jesus' parables reflected this same passion for the poor, widows, orphans, and outcasts. Jesus manifested the heart and mind of God.

God's wisdom and power were displayed by empowering the weak (especially for the Corinthian Christians). God had chosen them, not because they were powerful—but because they needed to be loved. God also chose them to prove to the rest of the world that something good can come from weakness. God wanted to prove that love can come from sinful people. God wanted to prove that people, when given a chance, can be holy.

The crucifixion of Jesus is the wisdom/power of God. To be humiliated in order to transform others seems insane to some people (1:18). However, this was the way of God. Jesus told his disciples that:

> If anyone wants to come after me, they must deny themselves and take up their cross every day and follow me. The one who wants to save their life will destroy it, but the one who destroys their life for my sake will save it. Will someone profit if they gain the whole world and destroy or forfeits themselves? The one ashamed of me and of my words, the Son of Man will be ashamed of them when he comes in his glory and the glory of the Father and of the holy angels. I tell you that there are some standing here who will not taste death until they see the kingdom of God. (Luke 9:23–27)

Carrying the cross did not mean that we have a burden to take in life. Carrying the cross did not mean that we make sure we are miserable in life. Carrying the cross means that we imitate Jesus. It means we accept the humility/humiliation of Jesus, who was called the "friend of sinners. . ." (Luke 7:34). Jesus ate, spent time, and talked to sinful people. He touched people with contagious skin diseases, talked to women (which men did not do in that world), held children, and helped people with demons and afflictions. He associated with people that religious leaders avoided. To carry the cross meant that his disciples are to follow the ministry which associated with and empowered the oppressed.

When I hear that someone is "humble" it usually means that they are very quiet, calm, and refuse any credit, praise, or complements. In some cases a person may express self-loathing ("I am unworthy," or "Only God is great and I am nothing."). While this may be our common understanding of humility it does not capture the meaning of the biblical words for humble/humility/humiliation.

The Hebrew and Greek words can refer to a class of people, rather than just a personal attitude. The words represent those who are poor, oppressed, outcasts, and suffering in society. In the kingdom of God humility was social rather than psychological. To be humble/humiliated not only meant that one had been oppressed it also reflected the people one associated with. For Jesus to be humble/humiliated not only referred to his oppression, but those he associated with.

> Do nothing from strife or conceit, but in humility count others more significant than yourselves. Let each of you look not only to your own interests, but also to the interests of others. Have this attitude among yourselves, which is yours in Christ Jesus:
>
>> though he was in the form of God, did not count
>> equality with God a thing to be grasped,
>> but made himself nothing, taking the form of a
>> servant, being born in the likeness of men,
>> being found in human form,
>> he humiliated himself by becoming obedient to
>> the point of death,
>> even death on a cross.
>
> God has lifted him up and given him the name that is above every name, so that at the name of Jesus every knee should bow, in heaven and on earth and under the earth, and every tongue confess that Jesus Christ is Lord, to the glory of God the Father. (Phil 2:3–11)

Christian humility did not refer to a psychological attitude of an individual. Socially it suggested that Christians embraced and identified with those marginalized in society. Rom 12:16 suggested that Christians were to "associate with the humiliated."[9] Like Jesus they associated with the poor and oppressed and sometimes defended their rights. The wisdom of God in Jesus' empire was not displayed only in the educational circles—it was manifested in the streets and slums of the cities.

Those in the church see that this wisdom and power comes through the Spirit. While there is a wisdom that can be gained by education, experience, and training; it is not the same as that which comes from the Spirit.

---

9. For a further explanation of this concept see: Ron Clark, "Associating with the Humiliated: Using Victim's Testimonies to Teach Religion to College Students in an Academic Setting," *Journal of Religion and Abuse* 7:1 (May 2005).

The Spirit teaches us the deep truths and will of God. The Christian reads the Bible, spends time in fellowship with other Christians, and practices acts of love and compassion for others.

There was also a contrast between the world's view of power and wisdom as compared to God's view. God empowers the weak to transform and change their lives. The world empowers the strong to stay in power. In the Roman world honor was a precious commodity. So was power. Power provided one with honor. Honor was power. Men lived in a world where honor was similar to America's credit rating. Those with high credit had power to get what they want. We work hard to build credit. Credit is our ticket to happiness.

Likewise, honor was an ancient person's ticket to happiness. People gained honor by taking it from others. A teacher rebukes another teacher in public and wins a debate. He gains honor but the other loses it. When Jesus stumped the Pharisees and Sadducees he was gaining honor, but they lost honor.

> Now we understand why religious leaders killed Jesus. They felt powerless and they tried to get even. They were afraid of being vulnerable.
>
> Now we understand why people struggled in the ancient world. They felt powerless. They were also afraid of being vulnerable.
>
> Now we understand why people struggle for power, honor, respect, or credit. They want and need power. They are afraid of being vulnerable.
>
> God is vulnerable;
> > Jesus loves,
> > Jesus dies,
> > Jesus continues to be rejected.
>
> It seems foolish but it is the way of God. It is the way of *agape*.
> > For some strange reason we struggle for success, power, and honor as well.
>
> Maybe it is because we are afraid to be vulnerable.
>
> We need a better way.

Paul told the church that the agonistic world was empty (1:28), passing away (7:31), and will cease (13:8). The rulers in this world could not understand God's ways (2:8). There was no need to struggle for honor or power. There was no need to humiliate others. God's honor was not acquired—it was given. You can't lose honor. You can only let someone else take it from you. That is what Satan likes to do.

Honor is given by God because we are chosen. It is free because Jesus struggled on the cross. We have honor, value, and are important to God. The world was struggling and looked down their noses at the outcasts. The outcasts were not strong enough to struggle so they gave up, didn't try, rolled over, and served the powerful. But the struggle for power was in vain. It is not there—it is gone—God has it. Earthly power in the Roman Empire was an illusion.

- God gave it to the outcasts, because they needed it.
- God shared it with those who identified with suffering.
- God blessed the dishonorable and gave them power.
- The rest didn't understand.

How could they? They were struggling for their own power which had blinded them to the way of *agape*. Paul explained to the church that they had no need to struggle for honor—it wasn't found in struggle. It is found in Jesus—the one who suffered, the one who chose not to fight, and the one who was humiliated and murdered.

The city of Corinth struggled to be accepted by Rome. They fought for attention and won. Therefore they boasted in themselves. They flattered the powerful ones hoping that these nobles would throw them a "power bone." They should have shared power with the majority of the population—the outcasts. But the struggle with the powerful only made them slaves.

The outcasts were the ones chosen by God. They were the ones given the chance to be something honorable. We believe that Paul's greeting to the Romans, in Rom 16:1–16, was written from Corinth. He mentioned Erastus and Quartus as important helpers. These were slave names. However they were public officials. Corinthian archaeologists have uncovered a piece of pavement dedicated to Erastus, a city official. This may be him. He may have been a slave who worked his way up and did well for himself. However, he too was chosen by God. In 1 Cor 16:17 he mentioned Fortunatus, and Achaicus. These were also slave names and we think that they were the ones of Chloe's house (1 Cor 1:11). It seems that some of Paul's buddies were slaves and public servants. It seems that they were part of the outcast group.

They must have been God's buddies as well.

Paul reminded the church that their Savior understood what it meant to be an outcast. However, the power of the Gospel was not through great speeches, military power, and wealth. The power rested in weakness, transformation, and by hanging out with common people. This was God's wisdom and the way Jesus chose to manifest glory, honor, and love.

The leaders of that age and the temporary empire could not understand this, because they did not have God's Spirit. However, since the Corinthian Christians had God's Spirit they should be able to understand. They should know. They should be able to comprehend what it means to be lost, to be on the margins, and to need acceptance. Unfortunately some in the church struggled to understand because they were immature.

This is why they were divided.

An Empire of the Spirit

1 Cor 2:6–30

> But we speak a mature wisdom, not a wisdom of this realm or from the rulers of this realm which is being abolished. We speak God's wisdom in a mystery of that which has been hidden. God saw ahead from this realm to his glory
>
>> The rulers of this realm did not know
>> If they would have known they would not have crucified the Lord of glory.
>>
>> It has been written
>> "Eyes have not seen nor ears heard and man's heart has not understood
>> What God has prepared for those who love him."
>
> But God through the Spirit has revealed these things to us. The spirit searches all, even the deep parts of God. The human spirit knows the human and the things of the human
>
> So it is with God's spirit, which understands God. We don't have the spirit of the world, we have received the spirit of God to know the gifts given by God. We do not speak in

> human teaching with wise words—we speak in spiritual teachings, not by human wisdom.
>
> The human soul does not receive God's spirit because it is stupid to them and they don't know how to judge spiritually. But spiritual people understand all things and are not judged. For who knows the mind of the Lord, or can confirm God?
>
> But we have the mind of Christ.

In this section Paul described three points concerning their relationship in the empire of Jesus. *First, it was an empire of the Spirit.* The Spirit knew the mind, thoughts, and plans of God. In the ancient world people existed as flesh, spirit, mind, and emotions/heart. Jesus told a lawyer that he needed to love God with his heart, soul, and mind (Matt 22:37-38). Paul prayed that Christians be made holy in Spirit, soul, and body.

> Now may the God of peace sanctify you completely, and may your spirit, soul, and body be kept blameless at the coming of our Lord Jesus Christ. (1 Thess 5:23)

The Greeks, however, made distinctions between the body and the soul. Since they felt that the body was not able to live in the heavens, the spirit or soul was distinct. It was an alien while on the earth and longed to be with the gods in the heavens. They began to emphasize living by the flesh separate from the spirit. The abuses of this belief system allowed some to satisfy their fleshly passions while believing that their spiritual life was not affected. This is very similar to American's belief that one can have a personal life separate from public life. Today we would call this two faced, hypocritical, or living a double life. However, some of these ancient people felt justified in satisfying their passions while claiming to be spiritually pure, not unlike some people today.

Romans were less likely to embrace this lifestyle. Romans saw the public sphere as an extension of one's private or family life. How a person behaved at home was seen to affect how they behaved in public. However, at the time of Paul and in the city of Corinth, the Greek culture had heavily affected the Roman ideals of life and morality.

Early Christianity believed that God was one, but in essence was spirit, mind, and messiah. As early as the second century the word "triad" was used to describe God as Father, Son, and Spirit.[10] This "triad" eventually became known as the Trinity. The belief was that God the Father is ruler of the world, Jesus is God (John 1:1); and the Spirit (since it represents the mind of God) is also God. God is manifested in these ways but God is one. The early Greek Christians eventually became nit-picky about the nature of Jesus and focused heavily on defining his humanity. A very complex doctrine of Jesus developed, yet many seemed to miss the simple point that God is one.

The same was true of humans. To focus on the distinctions between flesh, spirit, and soul is a moot point. Paul, in this Corinthian text, suggests that the Christians are either of God or of the world. They either live in the empire of *agape* or the *oikoumenē*. God's Spirit was active in revealing God's nature to the Christians. Paul mentioned that the Spirit reveals the mind and will of God because it knows God. To have the Spirit meant that one lived like God in the world. The Spirit helps us in our weakness and intercedes for God (Rom 8:26).

Not only was this an empire of the Spirit, *Paul suggested that God's Spirit was within them.* While the Greeks believed that the body could not house the divine Spirit Paul believed that the body was the place to glorify God (6:20) This was a reset button for the Christians. God chose and called them to be holy and they had been given the Spirit and the mind of Christ. Their divisiveness and emphasis on human wisdom came as a result of their life under the empire of power. However, they were in a new empire which was led by the way of *agape*. They were a new creation and were called to a different way. Their community, as a body, was to glorify God. The Spirit was there to give them the mind of God/Christ so that they could see the way of *agape*.

Paul encouraged them to act differently, not by threats but by love. Their calling and indwelling of God was their reset button. They could change direction because they were being led differently than the world. Their values and priorities were changing as Jesus transformed them. Rather than telling the Corinthian Christians that they were acting "badly" Paul reminded them that they were good, special, loved, and under a different empire. He also reminded them that the body could honor the divine Creator.

---

10. Theophilus, *To Autolycus*, 2.15. Clement of Alexandria, *The Stromata*, 5.14.

The majority of those called were not part of the "wise classes." God was going to shame the wise through them. This is known as divine reversal. God has always intervened in our world to choose the weak and dishonored in order to bless them and be glorified. Divine reversal occurs as God intervenes in order to reverse a system or culture. God intervenes to take power from the mighty and gives it to the powerless. In 1 Corinthians Paul reminded the church that God's divine reversal happened in the crucifixion of Jesus and the establishment of the Corinthian church. It is a pattern throughout the Bible.

- Older son serves the younger = Cain/Abel, Esau/Jacob, Ephraim/Manessah
- Outcasts are saved = Alien Egyptians accepted with Israel in the wilderness
- Barren women give birth = Elizabeth, Hannah, Sara
- A virgin becomes divinely pregnant = Mary
- A small nation is chosen by God = Israel

Jesus suffered the humiliation of the cross to bring honor to God and give hope to the humiliated. God became vulnerable to win those who needed hope and help. This is a message of power, not weakness. If the world considered God weak, because God sought relationship, then the world has the problem.

God's Ways

Today God still interacts with our world. First, *God's ways are many times foreign to how we normally live life.* If our life involves getting ahead, getting even, pay backs, isolation, independence, self-reliance, and material posessions then it is part of the *oikoumenē* which is "passing away" or "being destroyed" (1:28; 2:8).

God's way, the way of *agape*, involves relationships, love, second (or more) chances, empowerment, giving, and vulnerability. This is "weak" according to many in our world. The executive who says, "No!" to their boss so that they can be a better parent or husband is part of the empire of *agape*. The person who values relationship over personal gain is also part of this empire. The woman who takes the street kid to lunch and gives an hour of her time to listen and offer her heart rejects the empire of power for the empire of *agape*.

Second, *we are to imitate God's ways*. God chose the weak to display divine power (1:26–31). This has always been God's plan. In the prophets God's glory was displayed by:

- Choosing Israel (Deut 6:4–11)
- Bringing the Jews back from captivity (Jer 16:14)
- Forgiving the rebellious nation of Israel (Ezek 18:32)

God always initiated love/*agape*. When people responded, transformation happened. Christians today must practice initiating unconditional love, acceptance, and empowerment. This requires us to be vulnerable just as Jesus became vulnerable. However, it involves faith, risk, and love. It also transforms lives because it reflects these same qualities.

We are called to imitate God by choosing the humiliated in society. This does not mean that we think "bad" of ourselves or that we "act lowly and humble." It means that we have a heart for the humiliated, oppressed, and hurting in our communities. Our churches and ministries must reflect this same passion for those God has also called.

Who are the humiliated?

Humility has more to do with our social relationships rather than an individual's view of themselves. Jesus practiced humility as a friend of sinners and tax collectors (Luke 7), by becoming human and suffering on the cross (Phil 2:1–11), and becoming homeless (Luke 9). Paul encouraged the Roman Christians to associate with the humiliated (Rom 12:16) which applied to the many poor members of their church. The Corinthian church consisted mostly of the poor and oppressed which required the wealthy and noble in the church to care for them. This was humility.

When Lori and I began the Agape Church of Christ we attracted college students who loved to invite the homeless to church. We quickly realized that we would either hold these kids back or lead them. To lead them required courage and a willingness to be vulnerable. Since then Agape has focused on the poor, abused, those struggling with addictions, and now those in the sex industry. However, many young professional people have joined us who are not part of that segment of our community. Others work with the oppressed as a vocation and need affirmation for their struggles. They show humility by developing relationships with those who are oppressed. This is the humility of Jesus. This was what Paul wanted the Corinthians to practice. It is also what he has called us to be.

At the beginning of the twenty-first century Christianity is declining in the rich wealthy United States of America but experiencing explosive growth in South America, Africa, and Asia. The church grows in poverty, suffering, and disease. Christianity provides relief for those suffering and seeking hope. Research on church growth in China suggests that even thought the church is persecuted and exists underground, it is exploding in numerical growth and establishing new congregations. Christianity there provides hope and courage in the midst of persecution, suffering, and torture.

There is a reason that churches decline amidst affluence. Paul's point in 1 Cor 1:26–2:5 was that the Christians at Corinth must recognize that God called those who were nothing to be glorious, so that God may be glorified—rather than us. Christians are not called to create social networks only among the elites of society. They are called to associate with the humiliated and oppressed of society. While some call this the Social Gospel Paul would call it the Gospel. While some are ashamed of this ministry Paul was not.

Frederick Nietzche was a nineteenth-century German philosopher who was very critical of religion, especially Christianity. In his tract *The Antichrist* he stated:

> When everything necessary to ascending life; when all that is strong, courageous, masterful and proud has been eliminated from the concept of a god; when he has sunk step by step to the level of a staff for the weary, a sheet-anchor for the drowning; when he becomes the poor man's god, the sinner's god, the invalid's god par excellence, and the attribute of divinity—just what is the significance of such a metamorphosis? What does such a reduction of the godhead imply?[11]
>
> Not their love of men but the impotence of their love of men keeps the Christians of today from—burning us.[12]

He despised the German churches for working among the poor. He suggested that Christianity's weakness was its outreach to those he felt were

---

11. Nietzsche, *The Anti-Christ*, 33.
12. Ibid., *Beyond Good and Evil*, 84.

weak minded and to the lower class. Yet, this is exactly why the church grows. We were called by God to transform and bring glory to Jesus. That is God's glory.

Anton LaVey, founder of Satanism and heavily influenced by Nietzsche, also suggested that Christianity's call to humility was something to be rejected in our time.

> "Love one another" it has been said is the supreme law, but what power made it so? Upon what rational authority does the gospel of love rest? Why should I not hate mine enemies—if I "love" them does that not place me at their mercy? Is it natural for enemies to do good unto each other—and WHAT IS GOOD? Can the torn and bloody victim "love" the blood-splashed jaws that rend him limb from limb?[13]

While Christianity and the church have been seen as hypocritical, irrelevant, and weak, the truth is that this may be more a reflection of the modern church. However, when the church engages in social justice and chooses to empower the weak, humiliated, and oppressed, God is glorified.

Paul reminded the Christians that they were called to something greater than themselves. Paul told them that they were called to have the mind of God (2:6–16). This was revealed through the Spirit. For Paul, God was one. God was Father (who seeks relationship and chooses humans), Son (who shows us God in the flesh), and Spirit (who reveals God's nature). The Spirit reveals God's nature and desire to us. The Spirit helps us to grow and mature, so that we can be what God wants.

Too often, we claim to be sinners, sinful, flawed, or weak. This was true once in our lives. The call of God (1:26) was to lead us out of sin and into a new way of life. The Spirit works with us to help us become like God. God is love and to mature means to practice God's love. The Christian matures by accepting the leading of God's Spirit. This means that we repent and put away the sins that destroy ourselves and others. We learn to love others and call the weak into the Kingdom. We do not become arrogant but loving. To have the mind of Christ means that we understand God's love to us and others and that we practice it in our lives.

---

13. LaVey, *The Satanic Bible*, 32.

Power and the Emerging Culture

In this section of the book Paul suggests that the power of God is foreign to a world using power over others. A world like the Roman Empire that abused and withheld power did not understand a God who became powerless, vulnerable, and dishonored in order to save people. An emerging culture which uses power to isolate, segregate, and marginalize people cannot grasp the power of the Spirit which seeks to accept, embrace, and unify marginalized people. A culture which resists vulnerability cannot identify with a crucified Messiah. People who desire power as a tool to help themselves, will pass away, but those who empower others live on. Those who dispense condemnation will fade. Those who practice *agape* will remain. For Paul people, cultures, and communities that misuse power are the reason that Jesus is crucified even today. While the crucifixion of Jesus happened once 2000 years ago, he is daily crucified when men and women oppress others.

Today our society continues to oppress not only Jesus but Jesus' family. In Matt 25:40 Jesus called the outcasts of society "the little ones, my brothers [and sisters]." Men, women, and children are bought, sold, and trafficked in many countries throughout the world. Yet we in America are completely unaware that this happens in our front yard, our back yard, and in our homes. Women, boys, and girls are treated as sex objects in dark rooms, shady hotels, and in someone's home. Countless numbers of humans scan the World Wide Web hoping to see naked flesh, not caring what age person they see.

Men physically abuse their partners every day. Males continue to create an environment of entitlement and oppression towards females and other men who are not "masculine." This too is driven by men, male entitlement, and oppression of the weak. Physically and mentally handicapped people struggle to gain a sense of dignity, respect, and honor. They live in a world that is not always handicapped accessible. They see us roll our eyes when we realize that we picked a place to meet that has many stairs. I'm ashamed to say that I preached in a church that waited five years to put a ramp in our auditorium by the stairs. For five years those in wheelchairs complained that they couldn't get to the bathrooms.

> Five years!
> I never preached a sermon about it!
> Five years!

In order for change to happen in this illusory world, a permanent empire must be the catalyst for that change. In a world where people (mostly males) use other people and worship things/materials the only hope for change is to lead in *agape*. The challenge for the church is to be and model the better way.

- Every Christian who looks at internet pornography, pornography, strip clubs, or prostitution feeds the industry and empire of power, lust, and oppression.
- Every Christian who mistreats their spouse, partner, or family destroys any hope that we can change.
- Every Christian male who treats females as objects of lust, disrespect, and selfish gratification rather than equal partners in the image of God, destroys the power of *agape*.
- Every Christian leader who leads by fear rather than love manifests the temporary empire. They will not last in God's empire.
- Every Christian who dehumanizes and neglects people outside the empire of Jesus suggests that the church is less than the way of the world.
- Every Christian who turns their head to the oppression of the poor, weak, disabled, or aliens (illegal or legal) humiliates their Messiah.

Churches continue to withdraw from the dark sections of our cities, institutions, and communities. Because of this we focus on issues that affect only the rich, wise, powerful, and elite. Yet thousands suffer oppression, discrimination, exploitation, addictions, low self esteem, and guilt. Those are the people whom God chooses. Paul was able to write "not many of you were wise . . ." suggesting that many were from the lower classes of society. Yet the few who were wise continued to practice the ways of the *oikoumenē* by forming and encouraging alliances and human boasting.

When we first launched Agape we were asked what "group" we were "targeting." Church growth literature suggested that churches determine a "target group," which consisted of the people "we hope to attract." I find that in most cases target groups were white middle/upper class suburbanites. At least these are the ones with whom we focused our ministry.

We thought we knew our target group. We were wrong. We began to minister to the oppressed because Lori and I had been leaders in our community in domestic abuse and those who were marginalized in Portland. God led the people from Corinth to us. We found out that God's target group was not ours. In fact we found few churches actually targeting God's target group. As God told Paul, "I have many people in this city," while he was in Corinth, so God tells us, "I will send them; you just go and minister to them." God's target groups are the ones whom the *oikoumenē* rejects. Paul learned that those God chooses are different than he, a former Pharisee, would have chosen. Our response is to accept, love, and empower God's target group.

The empire of power chose its own people. They thought that they ruled the world. They were wrong. A preacher came to Corinth and began to minister to the people most unlike him. These were the people excluded, exploited, and evicted from the city and its power. They were the powerless. Paul was even one of them. While his education and Roman citizenship gave him status, he was allowed to mingle with the elite in society. However, he chose to be among the oppressed and work with his hands. God sent Paul to display the power of the Spirit so that they could be empowered to bring glory to God. This happened through *agape* rather than the fading power of a dissipating empire. The key to this transformation is the practice of love and acceptance of those in God's target group.

A MODEL FOR THE EMPIRE OF AGAPE

The humiliation of Jesus suggests that the incarnation involved a different type of power. Humility is less an attitude than an association. If the church is to practice humility, then it must go to those on the margins; the humiliated of our society. In the early stages of the Agape Church of Christ we began to reach people on the margins. One Sunday during a sermon, which typically is in a dialogue format, one young woman asked how Jesus could understand what it was like to be sexually abused as a child. It hit me at that point that Martin Luther was correct when he stated that in the crucifixion Jesus identifies with us in our humiliation, shame, and suffering. I had spent years suggesting that we overemphasize the crucifixion to the neglect of the resurrection. I still believe that the church continues to do this, however I realized that the crucifixion provides an identity with those carrying shame, guilt, and pain in their lives.

Rather than try to identify with Jesus' pain alone, the church should identify with God's humiliation. By becoming like Jesus we become vulnerable through a willingness to risk relationship by practicing love and acceptance, initiating relationships, practicing hospitality, and associating with the powerless of society. To be powerless is to be vulnerable and open to the effects of evil. As Hans Boersma once wrote, "Absolute hospitality not only makes it possible for the devil to come in . . . it makes his arrival unavoidable."[14] To empower the vulnerable and powerless is to empty ourselves. To empty ourselves is to become less like the *oikoumenē* and more like God. To become like God is to be mature. This is the foolishness of the crucifixion. This is not the way of the "fading empire." This is the wisdom of God. This is a way that the world cannot understand. It is the way of *agape*.

Paul suggested a better way. He suggested a better empire. He suggested a better leadership. We are capable of this. This can change the way of the world. However, we must be willing to embrace the humiliation of the Messiah as well as the humiliation of others. We must be willing to go to those who are oppressed. We must avoid seeing God's target group the way those in the *oikoumenē* see them.

> To them it is stupidity.
> To God it is wisdom.
> To us it is the way of *agape*.

---

14. Boersma, *Violence, Hospitality, and the Cross*, 237.

2

Power to the Powerless

1 Cor 3:1–23

Even I, brothers and sisters, am not able to speak to you as spiritual but as fleshly,
as babies in Christ.

I gave you milk, not food, but you still need this drink, you are not yet able to have this, and still not able:
> because when you have jealousy and bickering you are fleshly and you walk as humans.
> because when some say:
>> I am Paul's
>> or others say I am Apollo's.

Aren't you being human?
Who is Apollos?
Who is Paul?
> Ministers to those who have believed and each given by the Lord.
>> I planted.
>> Apollos watered.
>> God brought the growth.
> It doesn't matter who watered or who planted, God causes the growth.

The one who plants and the one who waters each gets their own reward according to their work.
We are God's co-workers,
> God's field,
> God's building.

IN THIS SECTION PAUL suggested that the root of the Corinthian problem was immaturity. While he earlier mentioned that they had God's Spirit (1 Cor 2:12) and that they were capable of understanding God's ways (2:16), here he challenged them for neglecting this gift. He told them that they were fleshly and immature (3:1). Their jealousy and fighting had stunted their spiritual growth by disrupting the harmony that Jesus had established.

Paul discussed the tension that existed between being in a fading empire and an empire of love; between living in the flesh, as human products of Corinthian/Roman culture, and spiritual life as residents in Jesus' empire. Because the Christians were forming human allegiances, Paul suggested that they were spiritually immature.

Their immaturity and worldliness were not only due to their human alliances. The root of their jealousy and strife lay in their acceptance of societal measurements of people in the culture. As mentioned in the last chapter, the empire of Jesus was driven by a counter-cultural view of people. While many ancient cultures honored those elite, educated, and wealthy; the Gospel provided salvation to the rest of the economic pyramid as well. Those people who were oppressed by the powerful became the ones who could identify with a humiliated God in Jesus. Preaching the dishonor and shame of the crucified Savior suggested that the power of Christianity was manifest by empowering the powerless.

While this would have been offensive to the elite, those who embraced this concept had no reason to form alliances, and boast about their leaders. Paul gave the example of his team's leadership style when he described their ministry with terms that would have brought criticism from upper-class community leaders. As mentioned earlier Roman society held common laborers in suspicion. To work with one's hands was a sign of poverty and lower class ethics.[1]

BLUE COLLAR WORKERS FOR JESUS

Paul referred to Christian leadership as farming, construction, and servants. First, Paul suggested that the Christian leaders were *farmers* (3:1–9). Farming was considered a dirty job and done by slaves or those hired to work their fields. Paul used this terminology not only because it was a common analogy for many in the church, but also to remind the

---

1. Jeffers, 24–25.

elite that he did not hesitate to associate himself with the lower classes. Paul mentioned that leaders, like farmers, worked together even though they may have differing farming techniques. God also worked with these *farmers* to fulfill one purpose—to cause the field to produce fruit. God's people were also compared to a field, vineyard, or orchard in the prophets (Is 5). The church, like the field, had one purpose—it was to mature and produce fruit for God.

Paul also wrote, "we are God's fellow workers, you are God's field, God's building . . ." He segued into this next thought with this statement. He compared the mission team to *carpenters/construction* workers (3:10–15). As with the farmers each had a different task but they all had one purpose. They were to produce a building that stood firm. This would be tested through natural disasters. Since Corinth was highly susceptible to earthquakes, the Christians would understand Paul's point as well.

In crowded Roman cities structural buildings were susceptible to fires, earthquakes, and other disasters. Ninety percent of people at Pompei lived in insulae which may be comparable to Corinth.[2] Augustus limited apartment buildings to seven floors due to the structural dangers that threatened the inhabitants. Many upper stories were wooden and weak. The Roman satirist Juvenal mentioned that the poor lived in the upper stories—a stark contrast to today.[3] Building contractors were judged by the soundness of their structures.

Paul suggested that the leader's work would be judged by the stability of their students. At Corinth, the leader's/teacher's/philosopher's worth was determined by the *public praise of his students*. For Paul, the longevity, spiritual growth, and stability of the disciples were a reflection of the leader's work. However, each leader was not responsible for the conduct of their students. God was the one who took responsibility. Paul reminded them of this.

> You are God's field,
>   God's building. (3:9)
> You are God's temple. (3:16)

Paul and the mission team wanted the Corinthians to understand that they were God's structure, not his. He wanted them to know that their leaders were facilitators for God, rather than gods themselves. Paul

---

2. Osiek and Balch, 31.
3. Juvenal, III.

was also concerned that they understood how serious division and strife worked in the body to destroy this structure.

> "If anyone destroys God's temple, God will destroy them. For God's temple is holy, and you are that temple." (3:17)

Paul emphasized that they had no right to boast and align themselves with male leaders. They were Jesus' people and needed to boast in that relationship.

> "Do you not know that you are God's temple and that God's Spirit dwells in you?...you are Christ's, and Christ is God's." (3:23)

In 1 Cor 1-2, Paul reminded them that their boast was in a humiliated savior. However, if they were to boast in men, their leaders must model the same humility.

1 Cor 4:1-13

> This is how one should regard us:
> > as servants/assistants to Christ
> > and managers of God's mystery.
>
> Managers have to be trusted, but with me it is a very small thing that I should be judged by you or by any human court. In fact, I do not even judge myself. I am not aware of anything against myself, but I am not found innocent. It is the Lord who judges me. Do not pronounce judgment before the Lord comes,
> > who will bring to light the things now hidden in darkness
> > and will disclose the plans of the heart.
> > > Then each one will receive their praise from God.
>
> I have applied all these things to myself and Apollos for your benefit, brothers and sisters, that you may learn by us not to go beyond what is written, that none of you may be puffed up in favor of one against another.
> > For who judges you?
> > What do you have that you did not receive?
> > If you received it, why do you boast as if you did not receive it?
> > > Already you have all you want!
> > > Already you have become rich!
> > > Without us you have become kings!
> > > > You should rule, so that we might share the rule with you!

> For I think that God has displayed us apostles as last of all, like men sentenced to death, because we have become a presentation to the world, to angels, and to men.
>> We are fools for Christ's sake, but you are wise in Christ.
>> We are weak, but you are strong.
>> You are held in honor, but we in shame.
>
> Until now we are:
>> thirsty
>> hungry
>> naked
>> beaten
>> homeless
>> we labor, working with our own hands.
>
> When mocked, we bless;
> when persecuted, we endure;
> when dissed, we encourage.
>
> The world considers that we have become, and still are nasty and scum.

Finally Paul suggested that he and Apollos were assistants or servants as well as house managers (4:1–13). Managers were typically slaves hired to act as foremen to manage the affairs of the householder. While this may have compared the two leaders to servants it suggested that Paul and Apollos had authority from God to care for body of Christ. The elitist attitude of the Corinthians suggests that the small portion of leaders from the upper-class may have been struggling to accept and unite with the lower social classes at church. It may also be that some of the elite, who used their hired servants, would have been humbled to have Paul identify with their servants. However, Paul soundly criticized them for their behavior. The apostles, their leaders, were marginalized occupants in this empire of power. The elite at Corinth were from this temporary empire.

Paul's concern seemed to be that the elite of the church were copying the behavior of the city, not Christ. Paul reminded them that he was their patron/father or spiritual leader.

1 COR 4:14-21

> I do not write these things to make you ashamed, but to challenge you as my beloved children.
>> Even though you have countless pedagogues/trainers in Christ, you do not have many fathers.
>> I became your father in Jesus Christ through the gospel.
>>> I urge you, then, be imitators of me.
>
> That is why I sent you Timothy, my beloved and faithful child in the Lord,
>> to remind you of my ways in Christ, as I teach them everywhere in every church.
>>
>> Some are arrogant, as though I were not coming to you.
>> But I will come to you soon, if the Lord wills, and will find out the power of these arrogant people, not their words.
>>> For the kingdom of God does not consist in words but power.
>> What do you wish? Shall I come to you with a rod, or with love in a spirit of gentleness?

Paul suggested that they had many pedagogues/trainers in their lives. Pedagogues were slaves hired by parents to train their children, who could become demanding and abusive. They could use fear and beatings with a rod to make these children obey. Paul alludes to this with his statement, "Shall I come to you with a rod . . ." Paul however would rather use love and gentleness. As a father or patron he claimed a position of ownership and authority over the Christians. However, it was a relationship of love rather than power and fear. This strong stance suggested to the church "If I am marginalized and I am your father/patron what does this suggest about you? What right do you have to boast?" It was similar to the statement Jesus made to his disciples:

> A disciple is not above his teacher, nor a servant above his master. It is enough for the disciple to be like his teacher, and the servant like his master. If they have called the master of the house Beelzebul, how much more will they abuse those of his household? (Matt 10:24–25)

Christianity is a reflection of the God we serve. The humiliated Messiah reminds us that our message, faith, and spiritual walk many times call us to a counter-cultural lifestyle. This does not always mean that we are constantly at odds with society. This suggests that we look to the Gospel as our theology for life. While the Romans laughed at a humiliated savior the Christians could only boast in him and those who practiced his ministry. Roman kings/emperors were glorified by their military conquests, power, riches, and wisdom. However Jesus as king/emperor was glorified through his death, humiliation, love, faithfulness, and power to create and reconcile life. Often I hear that Jesus was a warrior. While many verses in the New Testament suggest hat he conquers his enemies, the Bible also tells us he was:

- A slaughtered lamb/victim (John 1:29; Rev. 5:6)
- A humiliated victim (1 Cor. 1:18–24)
- A servant (Luke 22:27)
- A nurturer of the body (Eph. 5:27–29)
- An outcast (Heb. 13:12; 12:2)

Jesus as warrior was a stark contrasts to the Roman emperor as warrior, savior, and Lord. Jesus conquered through peace, love, and compassion. In a world of Roman power, violence, and fear the church must embrace the humiliated Messiah in order to effectively reach the people whom Jesus called into his empire. He is the great warrior and military commander—yet he is the prince of peace.

Currently Christians have had to do some serious soul searching. Many publications by Christian authors have suggested that North American and European societies deem the church irrelevant. Martin Luther King Jr. once wrote:[4]

> Things are different now. So often the contemporary church is a weak ineffectual voice with an uncertain sound. So often it is an archdefender of the status quo. Far from being disturbed by the presence of the church, the power structure of the average community is consoled by the church's silent—and often even vocal—sanction of things as they are. But the judgment of God is upon the church as never before. If today's church does not recapture the sacrificial spirit of the early church, it will lose its authenticity,

---

4. King Jr., *Why We Can't Wait*, 91–92.

forfeit the loyalty of millions, and be dismissed as an irrelevant social club with no meaning for the twentieth century. Every day I meet young people whose disappointment with the church has turned into outright disgust."

Not only was Dr. King an activist, he was a prophet. What he predicted has come true and today many young people question the value of the Christian community in our culture. Currently many church growth books have challenged the Evangelical church to realize that society sees us as irrelevant. American churches are facing a dilemma. The United States is quickly becoming one of the most unchurched countries in the world. Notice the following statistics:

- Previously 4,000 churches in America closed each year while less than 1,500 opened.[5] In 2006, however, for the first time in decades—more churches were started in America than closed.[6]
- U.S. churches are losing at least 3 million people a year to nonreligious lifestyles.[7]
- Fifty percent of U.S. churches did not record one conversion the previous year.[8]
- In 1965, thirty-nine percent of the U.S. was unchurched; in 2004, sixty-one percent was unchurched (unchurched is defined as having attended 0 or 1 times in the past year).[9] However, the Barna group estimates that in 2004 this statistic was only thirty-five percent.
- Sixty-two percent of America's 400,000 Protestant churches are declining in membership.[10]
- Eighty-four percent of American churches are growing at a slower rate than their community's growth rate which is twenty-one percent per year.[11]

---

5. Arn, "A Response to Dr. Rainer."

6. Stetzer and Connor, Research Report: Church Plant Survivability and Health Study.

7. Clegg and Bird. *Lost in America.*

8. Ibid.

9. Rainer, *Kairos Church Planting Summit.*

10. Ibid.

11. Ibid.

- Only twenty-nine percent (three out of ten) new members are assimilated (kept) in a church over a five year period.[12]
- Today's church is losing its grip on the very world it has been called to save.[13]
- Fifty-four percent of paid ministers have not shared their faith with an unchurched person in the past six months![14]
- "Only one out of three pastors—*pastors*—believes the church is making a positive impact on the culture."[15]
- Growing churches have pastors who believe in the Great Commission.[16]
- **Six out of ten Americans believe the church is irrelevant.**[17]
- Americans are not going to patronize an institution which appears incapable of living what it preaches.[18]

One response of the church has been to accept that we will always be at odds with our culture and expect those outside the church to judge us. However, since the 1960s church attendance has dropped drastically. Young people are leaving the church for the very same reason that society has judged us. The reality is that we are becoming irrelevant.

> The fact is, many churches have long abandoned any idea of reaching and influencing the city in which they are nestled, settling instead on some *reduced* vision that is much less intimidating. In this regard, Doug Small warns, "Pastors have given themselves to ministering only to the pain of their congregations but have failed to mobilize their congregations to minister to the pain and problems of the city. Either we learn to do both or reaching our cities for Christ will be nothing more than a hope and dream."[19]

Even worse, we are not becoming missional in our faith by reaching out to those who do not attend church or who do not know Jesus.

12. Ibid.
13. Lewis and Wilkins, *The Church of Irresistible Influence*, 17.
14. Rainer.
15. Lewis, 17.
16. McIntosh, *Biblical Church Growth*.
17. Ibid., 23.
18. Ibid., 40.
19. Lewis, 157.

Are Christians inviting non-Christians to church? The heartbreaking answer is no. Only twenty-one percent of active churchgoers invite anyone to church in the course of a year. But only two percent of church members invite an unchurched person to church.[20]

The question we must ask is "Are we reflecting the social justice values that the early church espoused?" Not only has Paul challenged the modern church concerning elitism, but Jesus modeled a life of social justice. The Gospel of Luke was a call to the established church to reexamine the Gospel story. Luke acknowledged that the stories of the life of Jesus were already circulated (Luke 1:1–4). He also made it a point to tell stories and quote Jesus concerning the poor, oppressed, outsiders, widows, and women. In Luke Jesus was the friend of sinners and tax collectors (Luke 5:29–30; 7:34). His first sermon concerned social justice as he quoted Is 61:

> He came to Nazareth, where he had been brought up. As was his custom, he went to the synagogue on the Sabbath day, and stood up to read. He was given the scroll of Isaiah the prophet. He unrolled the scroll and found the place where it was written,
>
> "The Spirit of the Lord is upon me,
> > because he has anointed me to proclaim good news to
> > > the poor.
> > He has sent me
> > to proclaim liberty to the captives
> > > and help the blind see,
> > to set the oppressed free,
> > and to proclaim the year of the Lord's favor."
> > > (Luke 4:16–19)

Later, when questioned by John the Baptist's disciples about his role as Messiah he claimed:

> When the men had come, they said, "John the Baptist has sent us to you, saying, 'Are you the one who is to come, or shall we look for another?'"
>
> In that hour he healed many people of
> > diseases,
> > plagues,
> > and evil spirits,
> > > and he gave sight to many who were blind.

---

20. Rainer, *The Unchurched Next Door*, 25.

> He answered, "Go and tell John what you have seen and heard:
> the blind receive their sight,
> the lame walk,
> lepers are cleansed,
> the deaf hear,
> the dead are raised up,
> and the poor have good news preached to them.
>
> Blessed is the one who is not offended by me." (Luke 7:20–23)

According to Luke, Jesus' came to free the oppressed and the poor. His ministry involved social justice and seeking those who were lost (Luke 15; 19:11). His ministry also would be offensive to others who saw religion as a spiritual retreat from the world. It would also offend those who ignored the lower classes of society. Luke's criticism was not just to the Jewish religious leaders of the day, it was also to the established church which seemed to have forgotten a major component of Jesus' ministry.

AN IMMATURE CONGREGATION

The Corinthian Christians were reflecting their culture's view of people by boasting about those who were elite and wise by the standards of the fading empire. The discrimination and elitism of this empire had entered the empire of Jesus and begun to tear apart the unity which Jesus had established. Paul's concern was that the church model the qualities of Jesus and himself as leaders. Paul maintained that Jesus was a humiliated savior in the eyes of this worldly empire. He also reminded them that he and the other mission team members were also outcasts in the fading kingdom.

Because of this the church had not matured and was not able to manifest the permanence and stability of the empire of love. They needed to love, practice harmony, and empower the weak. Since Jesus, Paul, and the team had invested this love in the church the Christians needed to mature by investing this same love to each other. This was the ministry of Jesus.

Social Justice Calls Us to Identify With the Oppressed

He sat across from me at Starbucks. He was over sixty years old, had two earrings, tattoos, and platinum blond hair cut in a Mohawk. We were having a cup of coffee at Pioneer Courthouse Square, a popular place in

Portland. This was where we met our first street kids. This is also where I first met Ken. Ken's story is interesting. He is an older man who left full time ministry in a large church, in North Washington, and moved to Portland with his wife to start a new church in the inner city with artists, musicians, and those disenfranchised from the church. I read his book They're Gentiles For Christ's Sake when we first started Agape in a home. I was impressed with what he and his wife had done. He is well known in Portland for ministry, compassion, and a radical love for the unloved. Every week they hold worship services and a meal under one of the Portland bridges and attract many street people. Ken calls it, "Our community."

As we talked he shared with me how they feed the homeless. Ken cooks the food so that it burns their mouth when they take a bite. I thought at first this seemed harsh but he leaned toward me and said, "Most homeless people get lukewarm or tepid food. To have it burn your tongue so that you have to move it around in your mouth is a privilege. It is a privilege of the middle class. We not only want to feed our people, we want to give them a sense of dignity." The more people I meet who work with the oppressed the more I learn that giving is about dignity. Not the giver's but the recipient's. As Ken emphasized to me over and over, "We want them to feel special." This is not only social justice; it is the way of Jesus, the way of *agape*.

Is this a unique ministry or is this the ministry of the modern church? Visit a Christian book store and peruse the shelves. What do you find? While these bookstores have done a wonderful job supplying us with many spiritual resources, they also reflect what many churches and Christians see as important issues in their walk with Jesus. What do you find?

- Proving God's existence
- Alternative Christian music
- Responsibly handling your finances
- Home school resources
- Doctrinal issues
- Weight loss programs
- Positive spiritual attitudes
- How not to divorce

- Men finding their true masculinity
- Women accepting their role in life
- Christian parenting

Are these the concerns of the elite or of those who live at the bottom of the social pyramid? Even more than this, many of these issues affect white middle-class Christians who live in America. In my ministry with common people they would suggest that we stock the bookshelves with spiritual books concerning:

- Showing God's love
- Dysfunctional marriages
- Domestic Abuse, Sexual abuse, trauma
- Eating disorders
- Poverty and homelessness
- Racism
- Single parenting
- How to encourage our children to be missionaries in the public schools
- Addiction/Recovery issues
- Male violence and sexism
- Pornography
- Human trafficking

It is interesting that many of these topics would not be in a typical Christian bookstore. Even more interesting is that these are issues that many secular corporations are addressing. Since we planted a new church my office has become Starbucks. They are very proud to publish literature concerning their commitment to ethnic diversity, social justice, global poverty, and how they plan to better address these in the future. However, when you visit a church what are the publications they offer you concerning their mission, vision, and values?

Evangelism means that we practice Jesus' ministry by bringing freedom and justice to all people who are oppressed, whether we consider them in or out of the church. This ministry must focus on justice issues that oppress any human being. Ray Anderson suggested that this social justice is an important part of evangelism.

> To separate evangelism and social justice as two issues to be debated and then prioritized is to split humanity down the middle. Theologically, it is a denial of the incarnation of God. In assuming humanity in its condition of estrangement and brokenness, Jesus produced reconciliation in "his own body," so that no longer can we see humanity apart from its unity in Jesus Christ. To approach persons in the context of their social, physical and spiritual existence, and only offer healing and reconciliation for the spiritual is already a betrayal of the gospel as well as of humanity.[21]

In the early Christian community social justice was an important mission of the church.[22] Christianity spread rapidly because the church worked with those at the bottom of the social scale, practiced hospitality, became an open family, and worked with the sick and outcasts.[23] However, the church also reached those who were influential in their cultures, who were encouraged to support, fund, and lead in this ministry to the community. This required them to change their views of people, power, and themselves. They were called to model a life of *agape* and practice this love in the church.

PAUL THE MENTOR FOR THE CHURCH

While Jesus' model of humiliation and vulnerability for people was displayed in the crucifixion, Paul suggested that this was to the glory of God and the transformation of people. Both Jesus and Paul modeled humiliation in society (4:9–13). However, as their mentor/patron/father/disciple Paul reminds the church today that we can be transformed by this love and identify with humility.

While we, like the Corinthians may respond to power, control, threats, and the many pedagogues who instill fear and obedience; Paul suggests that what we need is love, gentleness, and an accepting community. As a leader Paul was not afraid to be among the people and get his hands dirty. This was the mentor that they needed. The few Christians who were wealthy had no right to boast—their leader was a commoner.

---

21. Anderson, *The Shape of Practical Theology*, 203.
22. Clark, *Christianity and Roman Society*, 27–28.
23. Ibid, 27.

The lower-class also had no right to boast—their leader was not planning an overthrow. Paul called the church to work together to provide an accepting environment. This environment/empire was one of love, support, and encouragement.

Today the future of the church will not be determined by the size of its building, the amount of money used to fund its ministries, or the ability to connect with each generation. The future of the church will be determined by what it has always been. When the church empowers the humiliated to transform into the image of God it will last. When the church practices unconditional love with the "least of these," it will grow. When the church confronts the *oikoumenē*, it will become a lasting empire.

> Those who model the better way will always set the direction of the church.
> They will also lead the church to maturity thereby guiding the empire of power to peace.

3

Sexual and Social Power

SEXUAL POWER

1 Cor 5:1–13

I have heard that there is immorality among you, a kind not even accepted among the Gentiles, someone has his father's wife. You are puffed up. Shouldn't you be mourning so that the one doing this among you should be taken out?

Even though I am physically gone, my spirit is present among you. I have already judged this one who is doing bad things as though I were present. In the name of our Lord Jesus, when you come together my spirit is present with the power of our Lord Jesus. Deliver this one to Satan for the destruction of the flesh in order that his spirit may be saved in the day of the Lord.

It's not good that you boast about this. Don't you know that a little bit of yeast infects the dough? Clean out the old yeast in order that the new batch can be unleavened, because Christ is our Passover celebration.

Let's celebrate,
    not with old yeast,
        the one with evil and wickedness,
    but with good yeast,
        which is honesty and truth.

> I wrote to you in a letter not to associate with immoral people, I didn't mean those immoral in the world who are:
> greedy,
> thieves,
> idolaters,
> debtors
>> because you would have to come out of the world.
>
> Instead I wrote to you not to associate with one who names themselves a brother (or sister) who is practicing:
> sexual immorality,
> greed,
> idolatry,
> laziness,
> drunkenness,
> or a thief
>> don't even eat with someone like this
> Who am I to distinguish myself from those on the outside?
> You make a distinction with those on the inside.
> God judges those on the outside
> Take out the immoral person from your group

PAUL HAS RECEIVED A second report from the messengers in 1:11. The messengers indicated that one issue involved division and patron flattery in the church. This next issue involved sexual relationships. First, Paul mentioned that there was *porneia* (a Greek word that suggests sexual sin). *Porneia* involves adultery, sex outside of marriage, incest, prostitution, rape, and violations of sexual–ethical standards. The word is used eight times in 5:1–6:19. In the text above Paul indicated that a man was having sex with his father's "woman/wife." It could be any one of the following:

- He was having sex with his step-mother—his father can either be alive or dead
- He was having sex with his father's concubine/female slave—his father can either be alive or dead[1]
- He was having sex with a courtesan that his father owns or owned
- He raped any one of the above women

Roman law was concerned about "incest." Any of the above actions would have been viewed as incest in the Corinthian culture. The Jewish

---

1. de Vos, 208.

culture also condemned sex with an in-law, close family member, or concubine (Lev 18:6–7). Since the woman was not blamed for this action, by Paul, it may be that she has little to say in the relationship or that she was not part of the church. It may have been a relationship where the man used power over the woman to force her into a sexual relationship. This would be sexual abuse. It may be that the woman was not a Christian. This would be blaspheming the name of Jesus. However, Paul suggested that the offense was bad enough that outsiders considered it wrong.

Roman law strictly forbade incest in any form. This was a crime and was punishable through exile, fine, or in some cases death. Paul suggested that the church was boasting over this issue. It may have been that he was a wealthy patron whose "clients" were expected to praise him for his character. It seems that this noble man was guilty of manipulating people and forcing them to honor him—even though he was acting inappropriately. Paul criticized the church on two accounts:

- Even though they may have been subordinates to the man, the empire of Jesus called them to confront this man rather than praise him.
- His behavior was unacceptable both in the empire of power and the empire of *agape*. This called for confrontation concerning his sin because it infected the church.

The behavior of this man affected the woman as well as the rest of the church. She may have been a victim or she may have been a woman who saw that this Christian was like every other "horny" male in her city. Their acceptance (or refusal to condemn his actions) placed their reputation in jeopardy with outsiders.

In this section Paul seems concerned that the unethical behavior of this individual not only affected the church's reputation with outsiders, it affected the members of the church. In this letter Paul does not indicate that there was conflict between the church and the surrounding community (unlike Acts 18:12–17 when Paul was dragged before Gallio to defend himself). While Paul does not want the church to be influenced by their culture, he does seem to approve of their living in harmony with society. His analogy with yeast "infecting" an entire batch of dough suggests that this person's sin contaminated the rest of the church. The church was to be a safe place for people. In this case, a man may have been abusing power over others. If this was consensual sex the man was putting the community at risk of judgment from outside authorities. This was not the sin of the poor—it was one of the elite. The poor could not commit incest and live. Only those with money, status, and power can get away with incest. The church was also turning their heads to this issue.

Paul was grieved over this sin. He suggested that not only was Jesus present in the church, but he as well. The word for presence (*parōon*) is similar to the word used for the appearing of Jesus (*parousia*). Paul claimed to be present in spirit, suggesting that even in his absence his word was authoritative. In the Roman Empire Caesar lived in Rome, but his presence extended to all the colonies and cities controlled by Rome. He received reports from governors, generals, messengers, and foreign officials concerning each city in the colony. Roman temples in the cities reminded the citizens that Caesar was present. Paul used the same language with the Corinthian church. Even though sin existed in the church, he and Jesus were present and had both authority and influence on the congregation. Because of this, Paul suggested that they expel the man who was committing this sin.

When Paul challenged them to expel this man (5:13) he was quoting from passages in Deut (17:7; 19:19; 21:21; 22:21, 24; 24:7). In these texts the Jews were warned to keep a distance from those who worshipped idols, led the Israelites astray, were rapists, kidnapers, lazy, rebellious, drunk young men, and those who lied in court. Paul mentioned some of these in his list as well (5:10). Paul was concerned that the church become a safe place for people to grow and develop. He encouraged them to keep a safe distance from those who could harm them spiritually and emotionally. He was not suggesting that they withdraw from "the world" but from those among them who continued the practices of the empire of power and hurt others in the body. While Paul's comments about church discipline seem harsh to some, it was a common practice in ancient Corinth as well. In order for *agape* to reign in the hearts of people, the empire of Jesus needed to uphold their Lord's ethical standards.

Archaeologists have discovered fifteen lead texts from the temple of Demeter which contain curses for those who violated their group ethics.[2] These individuals were "handed over to the demonic world" because they were a threat to the community. Demeter was the goddess whose daugh-

---

2. Klauck, *The Religious Context of Early Christianity*, 224–25.

ter Persephone was kidnapped and raped by Hades. Her moving back and forth between Hades and her mother's place on Mt. Olympus was observed in the changing of seasons (winter = Hades and spring = Mt. Olympus). The cult of Demeter was a female based religion that believed in a distinction between good and evil; the demonic and divine. Curse tablets suggested that communities had codes of ethical conduct and expected congregations to be places that are safe from evil. The church likewise was to discipline those who threatened the safety of members.

While church discipline seems harsh to people today its purpose is to:

- *Restore honor to God and the church of Jesus.* People need to know that continually practicing immoral behavior is not acceptable by Christians. While some may not consider their behavior immoral, the church needs to define our moral convictions by communicating this to others. Instead of turning our heads to sin, Christians are called to confront sin in order to display holiness. Our world does not think we are hypocritical because we repent of sin—they think this because we turn our head to it.
- *Restore the sinner.* Paul reminds them that they are in a battle with Satan, not humans. Jesus is present in the body, not Satan. They are to confront this man and call him to a choice. Repentance is an opportunity for those in sin to change and work with their community to heal.
- *Reflect God's glory in our community.* Paul reminded them that they could judge those in the church. They do this so that the church can be pure, holy, and reflect the nature of God to the world. When the world sees that the church does not allow destructive, sinful behavior to go unchecked—people appreciate the church's presence.

Judging/Making a Distinction with Others

There has been tremendous emphasis placed on Jesus' statement in Matt 7:1, "Do not judge in order that you will not be judged." Another way to say this is "You all should not condemn, so that you won't be condemned." Some will suggest that we cannot challenge others on their sin because Jesus says, "Don't judge me." This has been somewhat of a trump card for people, and we don't know how to respond. However, Jesus makes a distinction between those who are submissive to his teaching and spiritual "dogs" or "pigs" (Matt 7:6). Jesus does make distinctions between those in the faith, and those who stubbornly refuse to follow him. Even more, there are people whose behavior potentially threatens men, women, children and their spiritual, emotional, and personal development. These people are dangerous especially when they enter a "family" and create an unsafe place for its members. However, there is no contradiction between Matt 7:1 and 1 Cor 5:12. "Are you not to judge/make a distinction those inside? God will judge those outside!"

- Matt 7:1 reminds the disciples that we will be judged with the same standard we judge others. We are to clean up our lives so we can see clearly to help others.

- We are called to be holy—not hypocritical. Hypocrites judge others before themselves. Jesus called us to judge ourselves first.

- In 1 Cor 5 Paul was speaking collectively. He reminds us to judge the inside, not the outside. Individually that is our own lives. As a church, that includes our members. Those who profess to be Christians are subject to peer evaluation in the faith. Just as you and I clean up our lives so we can help others, the church removes the "logs" out of the body in order to help others. We cannot guide those outside of the faith if we have members who continue to sin and hurt other people.

Proverbs tells us something about spirituality and group accountability:

> There is severe discipline for the one who forsakes the way; whoever hates being rebuked/corrected will die. Sheol and Abaddon lie open before *Yahweh*; how much more the hearts of the children of humans! A scoffer does not like to be rebuked/corrected; he will not go to the wise. (Prov 15:10–12)
>
> > Rebuke/correct one who has understanding, and they will gain knowledge. (Prov 19:25b)
> > Whoever loves discipline loves knowledge, but the one who hates rebuke/correction is stupid. (Prov 12:1)
> > The way of a fool is right in his own eyes, but a wise person listens to advice. (Prov 12:15)
> > Poverty and disgrace come to the one who ignores instruction, but whoever accepts rebuke/correction is honored. (Prov 13:18)

Spirituality and wisdom are displayed by a willingness to work with others to achieve a common goal. While I acknowledge that many churches, families, clubs, gangs, and groups manipulate and brainwash individuals, this does not mean that the faith community should not work as a group. It does not deny that an individual who goes against the group may be self centered and blinded by their own pride. We also must remember that there are many others, who do not name Jesus as Lord, who have the same passion and courage for morals and a safe environment that are similar to Christians. They too struggle with those self centered, blinded by their own pride, and those overcome with guilt, grief, and sin. In the faith community it is important to believe that God is working in the lives of others, even if they don't agree with us. Our reputation with them is equally as important.

I have been convinced of this the more that I work with local abuse agencies. Most are frustrated because the faith community has turned its head to these crimes against humanity. They are correct, we have. However, they have also become our cheerleaders in our fight to confront Satan in these dark areas of society. They have equipped us, taught us, mentored us, and fought with us. While we may have strong disagreements over some ethical issues we do agree that human induced trauma is one of the greatest forms of evil in our world today. They also agree that all people must fight this evil together by supporting, encouraging, and equipping others. I, like Paul, feel compelled not only to oppose this form of evil, but also to provide an example to my colleagues by training communities to also discipline those who practices this evil as our community would. Even more, if the church where I lead does not confront human induced trauma or turns its head to the abuse of others, I lose credibility in my community.

Spiritual discipline helps us in our growth with God. It also involves the faith community's encouragement and challenge to members to bring honor to God through their behavior and lifestyle. When members are guilty of sexual sin, physical and verbal abuse of others, arrogance, pride, drunkenness, addictions, stealing, dishonesty, violence, or other sins they bring shame to the name of Jesus. The group, many times, must call them to repentance.

We must bring honor to the name of Jesus. *First, hypocrisy dishonors God, Christians, and others affected by sin.* The high majority of people I encounter who have left church do not embrace Jesus' name, or claim to not believe in God, and have expressed to me that they were hurt by their church. Their abusive parents were active in church. A minister or youth worker sexually abused them or a friend. A preacher had affairs while preaching about purity on Sundays. Youth in a teen ministry were cruel and arrogant to others. Other youth in the church introduced them to alcohol, drugs, pornography, or sex. While I agree that we are responsible for our own faith choices, God will not tolerate hypocritical behavior in the church.

> You who boast about the law also dishonor God by breaking the law? As it is written: "God's name is blasphemed among the Gentiles because of you." (Rom 2:23–24)
>
> A son honors his father, and a servant his master. If I am a father, where is the honor I am supposed to have? If I am a master, where is the respect I am to have? (Mal 1:6)

Many times the choices of Christians affect the faith of others. When I read the Muslim Sacred Writing (*Koran*) or Anton LaVay's Satanic Bible, I clearly see how another religion began because of Christian hypocrisy. We are called to a life of holiness to bring honor to Jesus in our world.

Second, the church must confront those in sin and offer hope of restoration. Paul calls this expelling or handing them over to sin. 1 Cor 5 describes and extreme sin that the Corinthians obviously knew about and tolerated. Our first step is not to "kick someone out of the church." This is reserved to a hard heart, full of sin, rebellion, and pride that rejects our call to holiness. In many cases they have already cut themselves off from the body emotionally. In recovery ministry this is called intervention. Sometimes a person responds. Other times they reject our help. Either way intervention is the work of *agape*.

SPIRITUAL DISCIPLINE

Jesus gave a process to help a person stay connected to God. If someone sins against us personally we inform them and help them repent (Matt 18:15–20). If they reject us we take one or two others as witnesses for *spiritual intervention*. If they still refuse to repent we let the church (leaders) know. If they reject the leaders' advice then they have distanced themselves from Jesus' body.

Jesus wants us to try to help people stay faithful. This can only happen through relationships and support. I suggest that ninety eight percent of the people who become entangled with sin do so because they do not have a support group or accountability. We can show love and compassion when we meet face to face and tell people we love them and want to help. Very few will resist to the point of being expelled from a community.

Sometimes there exists an imbalance of power when a leader sins. Leaders who abuse their power over members have, through time, forced them into submission, caused them to leave, and/or damaged them spiritually and emotionally. Abusive spouses or parents spread fear to family members. Matt 18:15–20 does not usually work in these situations. We cannot tell the "little ones" to go show their brother or sister their fault because the relationship of power creates fear. A person cannot openly confront the other in this relationship because the sinful party is controlling and abusive. An imbalance of power requires an equalization of power from God's leaders.

In the Old Testament God never sent the poor, widows, orphans, immigrants, or oppressed to confront the abusive leaders. God sent the prophets. We cannot expect the oppressed to confront those in power. We must expect leaders to confront those in the church and those in our communities who abuse power over others.

In 1 Tim 5:19 the young evangelist was told to publicly rebuke elders/leaders who had sinned. He was told not to receive or accept an accusation unless it had been given by two or three people. This suggests that more than two people had come to Timothy with an accusation of a leader's sin. While we encourage people to go to others when they sin against them, leadership understands that some in power may be unapproachable. Leaders must support each other, but also be open to addressing the sins or abusive behavior of those in power.

Sacred Spaces

Paul did not want the Christians to keep a distance, from those caught in sin, outside the church. God will make a distinction with outsiders, not Christians. Christians needed to be strong enough to develop relationships and "eat" with those in the world who practiced sin. When the church is a safe place for people to grow and transform into the image of Jesus, outsiders can enter and develop as they wish. Paul maintained that the church was to be a safe place for transformation and growth.

One of the characteristics of newer churches, called Missional or Emerging, is creating *sacred spaces*. Creating these spaces means that the church moves into the secular community and develops communities that help others in their walk with God. It also happens when Christians develop spaces of influence in their community. Paul gave the Christians permission to associate with those who practice the behaviors listed in 1 Cor 5–6.

Too often Christians have focused time and energy on retreating from the world. Paul stated that he did not want Christians to disengage from the world (5:10). For Paul, the church must associate with, eat with, and interact with people outside the church regardless of their moral choices. Modern Christians have struggled with this permission for the following reasons.

First, *we have devoted so much time with Christians that we do not know or have relationship with unbelievers*. When we encourage Christians to bring unchurched friends to church I constantly hear, "I don't know any unchurched people." This may be true, however Jesus was not afraid to associate with "sinners and tax collectors" on a regular basis. Both Paul and Jesus were not afraid to push through their culture's table fellowship rules in order to mix with those who needed God (Luke 5: 31; 15:1; 19:7; Acts 18:6–7).

Second, *we have created such a distance from the unchurched that they feel manipulated when we try to share our faith*. This does not stem from a relationship with them but a forced presentation of Jesus' salvation story. They must first believe that Jesus is a friend of outsiders by observing its practice in the lives of Christians.

Finally, *we are afraid that by mixing with the "pagans" we might lose our faith*. However, we have only ourselves to blame. The Christian mission is to go to others, become the friend of outsiders, and share the God of *agape* to them. They cannot leave dead idols until they see a living, loving, and relational God in us. Therefore if we wish to fulfill this mission it is our responsibility to develop our faith and become strong enough in our faith to be able to share it where God calls us to go.

Paul compared his "spiritual strength training" to the Isthmian games (9:24–27). He suggested that he had disciplined his body to be able to preach to others and model a life of sacrificing so that others might be saved. The church today has permission to be among others who need

Jesus, healing, and transformation. However, we must be serious in developing our faith.

Will the church take advantage of this freedom?

SOCIAL POWER

1 Cor. 6:1–11

> Some of you dare to have your legal business taken to the unrighteous and not to the saints.
> Don't you know that the saints will judge the world?
> If you judge the world can't you also judge little things?
> Don't you know that we will judge angels and living things?
> On the one hand if you judge things in this life why not also the church?
>
> I say this to your shame.
>
> Isn't there someone wise or powerful enough to judge in midst of the brothers and sisters?
>
> But Christian takes Christian to court and this among the unbelievers.
>> Already you are defeated when you judge each other. Wouldn't it be better to have injustice or much more be cheated? But you are unjust and cheat your brother and sister.
>> Don't you know that unrighteous will not inherit the empire of God? Don't be deceived:
>
> - Neither sexually immoral
> - Nor idolaters
> - Nor adulterers
> - Nor the passive partner in homosexuality
> - Nor the active partner in homosexuality
> - Nor thieves
> - Nor greedy
> - Nor drunkards
> - Nor the lazy

- Nor those who take from others

These will not inherit the empire. Some of you were like this but were washed, made holy, and justified through the name of our lord Jesus Christ and by spirit of our God

Going to Court in the Ancient World

In Roman culture going to court was a nightmare—even more so than today. Lawyers were hired to humiliate and do whatever it took to win a case. Lawyers were excellent speakers and their job was to discredit any accusations and witnesses who attacked their "client." In Athens the cult of Dionysius (Bacchus—the god of wine) expressly forbade members from taking each other to court. One situation occurred when two of their members were involved in a drunken brawl with each other after a meeting (imagine being drunk at the god of wine's worship). They went to court against each other. The group disciplined them for taking a fellow worshipper to court.

Once again Paul was concerned that those outside the Christian faith were more spiritually mature than the Christians. Evidently, according to this text, Christians were either suing each other or having their grievances decided within the legal system. Paul's objection to this expressed his concern for unity.

- Only the wealthy could survive in court. This immediately established an oppression of those members who could not hire an attorney.
- Court was a humiliating experience. In 6:6–7 Paul's concern is that the Christians (or at least their lawyers) would tear each other down in public. This would happen in front of outsiders who were judges and observers of the Christian community. This would also suggest that love and respect did not exist in the body.
- This was also a challenge to leaders. In 6:3 Paul reminded the Christian leaders that they should be able to effectively mediate family issues. Going to court meant that the church had become uninvolved in this matter. As with the sin of sexual immorality (5:1–13) the church had neglected to help people. In 6:7 "already you . . ." suggests that the church had failed to help resolve issues among themselves.

While this text has been used to suggest that Christians should not go to court for any reason, I think it has deeper meanings. First, *Christians should be able to address these issues*. This does not apply to divorce settlements, abuse, insurance settlements, malpractice, bad business deals, or when one party refuses to compensate a person for their loss. When Paul says, "why not rather be wronged?" this does not mean that we are to let people take advantage of others. It does not mean that we should not stand up to corrupt institutions. Paul's point is that the church leaders need to be involved in reconciliation and resolving conflicts and disputes. Too often churches either ignore conflict with members or let other people work out their disagreements. Paul does not believe this. One example is found in the church at Philippi.

> I encourage Euodia and Syntyche to agree in the Lord . . . (Phil 4:2)

Paul believed that the faith community must help members resolve their own conflicts. There should always be an attempt to address injustice and compensate victims.

Second, *the public courts are not able to administer justice with the same grace as the church*. While American courts are more civil than ancient justice systems, it is still a shame when Christians have to use the legal system to enact justice. They do this because they feel helpless and that justice is blind. Justice should exist within the community. Usually one person is not willing to acknowledge wrong doing and validate the other. Paul believed that Christians needed to love each other and work together. There needed to resolution and peace in the family. When issues cannot be resolved the legal system may have to intervene—yet peace will not be established through the legal system. There may be satisfaction for one party but not peace.

Finally, *the legal system may be necessary to compensate or protect the victims but it rarely establishes love, forgiveness, and encouragement*. My wife Lori and I have spent many years helping those who have been through divorce. The custody and mediation hearings can be very painful to the spouses, the children, and other family members. It cannot establish *agape* because it is part of the *oikoumenē*. While divorce may happen, it is important that the church emphasize peace, even after divorce. We have taken such a stance against divorce that we have failed to talk about "peace while divorced." The legal process of divorce is emotionally and physically draining for people and the church needs to help couples heal and live in peace. This is especially true when children are involved. If reconciliation does not happen, peace must. Paul tells Christians that "God has called us to peace..." (1 Cor 7:16). Instead of taking sides Christians must try to cultivate peace, forgiveness, love, and reconciliation.

Preventive Justice

Since Paul mentioned this immediately following the sexual affair in chapter five, we may be able to conclude that this may refer to the same situation. Because the gentiles considered the offense incest it would seem logical that this was the court issue he mentioned in chapter six. Paul was concerned that the church had not taken this matter seriously. This may be the "boasting" that he mentioned in chapter five. He admitted that he wrote these comments to "shame" them (6:5 as opposed to 4:14 where he did not want to shame them). The church's refusal to litigate this issue had forced the community courts to address the matter. Paul suggested that there were people within the church who could mediate and judge the situation.

The Corinthian Christians were not willing to embrace those who were suffering because they were seeking the glory of men. Paul again mentioned a list of people who could not be part of the Christian community (6:9–11). The list is almost exactly the same as 5:11 except Paul added three other behaviors. Repetition always suggests that the author has continuity, but when something is also added to a repeated list, the author is trying to get the reader's attention. Paul added three words to his list:

- Adulterers = people who violate relationships that exist between a man and a woman. This involves sex with another man's wife, concubine, slave, or other female possession. Usually men committed adultery against another man. This case is similar to 1 Cor 5.
- Soft/male prostitutes/the passive, younger, feminine partner in a male same sex relationship.
- Homosexual offender/the aggressive, older male in male same sex relationships.

In the ancient world homosexuality was practiced but not completely accepted by mainstream culture. Roman philosophers condemned adultery, homosexuality, and incest. While the Greeks practiced bi-sexuality and cultivated older/younger male homosexual love, many Romans felt that the immoral ways of the Greeks had infected their Roman culture. Pederasty was commonly associated with athletic festivals and Corinth's emphasis on the games would have created an environment for this practice.[3] The Spartans encouraged this because they believed that men would fight stronger for their lover. They also encouraged the men to have sex with each other rather than waiting until they returned home to their wives. At Athens students gave many of their teachers sexual favors as a way of showing appreciation. While some Romans practiced homosexuality it was many times a way of humiliating those of the lower class. Young boys and girls were present at Roman meals so that when the guests became drunk they could indulge in sexual pleasures. The guests were the aggressors and the slaves always the passive partner. Sexual expression was many times practiced within a cultural honor system (the aggressor and the passive) where those who were passive were mainly slaves, those indebted to their superior, and young boys. Julius Caesar, Tiberius, Caligula, and Nero were well known for practicing bi-sexuality in their time. However, many philosophers spoke out against these practices.

When the Roman General Titus (before he became emperor) captured the beautiful Jewish queen Bernice, he had her live in his home as his partner. Titus tortured and beheaded many philosophers for speaking against this illicit relationship. Moralists and philosophers were not afraid to speak out concerning adultery, homosexuality, and bi-sexuality. Paul was no different. He also voiced his opinion; however he did it within a community.

Paul may be thinking of the sexual offender in chapter five when wrote 6:9–11. He does not say that those in the list have no hope of change; he suggests that God's empire does not give an inheritance to those who practice these sins. This "inheritance" theme is common in 1 Corinthians and refers to family membership and support.[4] Practicing these behaviors (which was different from struggling to overcome them) was unacceptable. While the *oikoumenē* embraced various sexual behaviors the empire of *agape*, like other philosophical communities called for change. Paul wanted them to know that rejecting the empire of *agape*'s ethical code meant exclusion from the church. He, by the authority of

---

3. Scanlon, *Eros and Greek Athletics*, 96.
4. Hellerman, *The Ancient Church as Family*, 101.

Jesus, called them to the values and ethics he had given them. The phrase "don't you know," (6:2, 3, 9, 15, 16, 19) in this chapter suggests that Paul was reminding them of key ethical statements he had given them before. As a mentor Paul, like God and many leaders in the *Torah*, encouraged them to remember that they were to be morally distinct from those in their communities. He also maintained that the empire of *agape* was different from the empire of power. However, Paul suggested that many of them had transformed from these lifestyles. Those who had been the sexual aggressor and those who had suffered as passive victims had changed. While many would have struggled with guilt and shame Paul reminded them that they were transformed. The allusion to "washing" reminded them of their baptism and conversion. The church was not a place to judge people; it was to be a safe place where people could transform into God's image. People are to be baptized into Jesus and a community that supports them in their life of *agape* and transformation from the temporary empire.

1 Cor 6:12–20

> All things are lawful for me but not all things are helpful
>
> All things are lawful for me but I am not controlled by them
>
> Food is for the belly and the belly for food
>
> But God will cause these to be abolished
>
> The body is not for sexual immorality but for the Lord and Lord for his body. The God raised the Lord and will also raise us up.
>
> Don't you know that your bodies are members of Christ. Shall I take members of Christ and make members of prostitute—no!
>
> Don't you know that if you cleave to a prostitute you are one body with them. The scripture says, "the two will become one flesh." The one joined to the Lord is one spirit with him.
>
> Flee prostitution! Other sins are outside the body, but sexual immorality is a sin against one's own body.
>
> Don't you know that your bodies are a temple of the Holy Spirit?
>
> You are not your own, you were bought with a price—honor God in your body.

Sexual Sin and the Church

In this text Paul challenged the notion that "everything is permissible." As mentioned earlier, this may have been a common saying for young men that life was about exploring excesses. In this case Paul refers to prostitution.

Sex is a joining of two bodies. The quote from Gen 2:24 was in reference to Adam and Eve's sexual union. The Hebrew term was "cleave" or "join." Sex between a man and woman is a beautiful thing, created by God, for humans as well as all creation. Sex can be pleasurable. Sex can be enjoyable. Sex can bring glory to God. Sex can help draw a man and woman closer together. Sex can also create new life.

Yet sex can also be painful. Sexual abuse is painful because the abuser violates the trust of another. Sex outside of marriage can place people in a vulnerable situation and destroy trust. Adultery can be painful because of the guilt that it brings on the guilty party and the pain it causes to the spouse who is violated. Pornography can bring sexual pain because the one viewing the material destroys self esteem and distances themselves from relationships. It also further continues to degrade women and feeds an industry designed to oppress rather than empower women. It damages future relationships and develops an addiction that is self gratifying and lonely. It causes shame in one's spouse, partner, and children. Prostitution further enslaves women, and men, in an institution created to abuse young women and tell men that they are only sexual creatures. It feeds the pocket of the pimp who exploits others for their own greed. Coerced sex is painful because it violates trust and destroys the soul. Sex is created to be pleasurable and experienced in a covenant relationship, but our culture has found a way to destroy and warp this wonderful gift of God. The *oikoumenē* sees sex as power and self gratification. The *oikoumenē* further complicates sexual or gender confusion by expanding the categories of gender as seen in the LGBTQQ categories.[5] The empire of *agape*, however, views sex and gender as a way to reflect Jesus' relationship with the church and empower the other spouse. For those who are single the empire of *agape* provides a place of acceptance and a community of support.

---

5. This means Lesbian, Gay, Bisexual, Transgender, Queer, and Questioning. These are common terms used to allow gender exploration and freedom to redefine one's gender orientation. I find that instead of guiding people in their struggles this seems to make the problem more complex and confusing. While many of the agencies we work with hold to this terminology it is important that the church take the opportunity to offer guidance and clarity to men and women struggling to find who they are, rather than condemn or further confuse them. Corinth would have had many men and women confused about their sexual desires, orientation, and nature. Yet Paul offers guidance, transformation, and a healing community of acceptance for these men and women.

This began in the Garden of Eden. The word for "naked" (Gen 2:24) is the Hebrew word *arum*. It is the same word for "crafty." In Gen 3:1 the devil/snake was craftier (*arum*) than all the creatures. Before the encounter with the devil humans were together, naked (*arum*), and not ashamed of it. After the encounter with the *arum* devil/snake, men and women became ashamed. The similarity between the shape of the naked phallus and the snake also suggest that sin came as a choice to respond to temptation through coercion. The naked and crafty phallus once again created distance between God and humans. Evil distorted the beautiful gift of sex and physical openness that God had given for humans to enjoy.

One of the earliest accounts of creation in the ancient world was a story called The *Epic of Gilgamesh*. In this account Gilgamesh decided to create human (man) as a friend. The man was a beast, savage, and animal. Gilgamesh decided to help this man become "civilized." He introduced the man to a prostitute and the man's "eyes were opened" and his "mind became free." In the ancient world sex, especially with a prostitute, was important for young men to become "civilized" men. However with God, this can destroy humans.

The myth of free sex continues throughout history. I remember as a young man watching the movie, *The Best Little Whore House in Texas*. The message was that men needed to have a brothel in their neighborhood to make them feel like men. The prostitutes were played by models, Dolly Parton was the Madam, and Burt Reynolds was the local sheriff who turned his head and allowed this institution to exist for the good of the community. Dom Deluise played the television evangelist who "mercilessly attacked these good hearted women and shut down their historic landmark." The other message was that religion (Christianity) was hindering the normal sexual and emotional development of men.

Yet this is not the message I hear about prostitution. I find that the message from prostitution is much different than that from Dolly Parton and her "girls." Now that we are working with human sex trafficking the research is astounding. In America we arrest the prostitutes and glorify the pimps. Anyone can go to a popular department store near the end of October and find "Pimp and Ho" costumes designed for young boys and girls. We live in a culture that glorifies "pimping" and judges "prostitutes." Prostitutes are usually young runaway females who are captured by men who enslave and exploit them sexually. Prostitutes are young girls kidnapped in other countries and sold to pimps on the black market. Prostitutes are young Indian girls sold to the priest and trained to treat sex with other men as a spiritual journey for an Indian goddess. Prostitutes are women who have addictions but find that being paid for sex provides food for their children or their addictions. Prostitutes are young boys and girls used to satisfy male pedophiles who are deeply disturbed. Prostitution is another form of oppression and enslavement for women and young boys and girls.

Prostitution is also damaging to men. Men who pay prostitutes for sex not only further oppress women; they allow themselves to become vulnerable. They let someone else control their sexual desires. They create an encounter that allows for emotional distance. They allow themselves to buy into the myth that for men sex is not about relationship, trust, love, and compassion. They allow their bodies, heart, soul, and mind to be controlled by sexual passion. Men do not grow from beast to civilized man in these sexual encounters—they return to primitive behavior. Prostitution, sexual addictions, affairs, and sexual encounters reduce men to beasts and exploit women and children. Sexual violence, domestic violence, addictions, divorce, adultery, depression, guilt, despair—these are many times part of this "exploration of sexuality" that I see encouraged by our culture. I have seen the damage that this does on marriages, families, and self esteem.

Yet we live in a culture that tells us that Christianity is hindering our rights to explore sexuality. If we could just throw off these puritan Christian values then we wouldn't feel guilty. Correct?

I remember when Jocelyn Elders, former Surgeon General, under former president Bill Clinton, felt that providing condoms in our high schools would help lower the teen pregnancy and communicable disease rate. Those who opposed this were seen as religious people with a sexual hang-up. Yet this never solved the problems of teen pregnancy or venereal disease. Why? Because this communicated to teens, usually young men, that everything is permissible. It communicated that "you cannot have self control when it comes to sexual issues, therefore we'll help you have sex safely."

I wonder if the problem existed in the minds of Baby Boomers (those born from 1945–1964). The children of the 60s wanted to explore sex and struggled to exhibit self control—so why shouldn't our kids do as we did? Instead of empowering our kids to practice self control (they do this in sports, band, school, and other areas of their lives) we gave them a license to give in. Since it is difficult we just say, "Everything is permissible."

This may be why Paul discussed the body in this text. Prostitution in the ancient world was very common. Many female slaves made a profession out of prostitution. Women slaves trained other women, including their daughters, to perform sex for money. They developed a profession that was seen as important to the city and necessary for young men or married men who were not "getting it" at home. Yet, this still existed in a culture that treated women with disrespect. Prostitution was not seen as a noble profession. Prostitutes were still treated with contempt. Prostitution existed because men were taught that sexual self control was not a noble quality or possible in men. Prostitution existed so that *men* could feel satisfied.

This was Paul's point. Prostitution damages bodies. While some of the Stoic philosophers believed that satisfying the body's lust could not harm the soul Paul believed that the body was a safe place for the soul. The body, according to Paul, could bring glory to God, who had created it for good. Sex, as a cleaving of bodies, is meant to be practiced in a covenant relationship. It is a cleaving of male and female, who in the Genesis text are compliments of each other (Gen 2:20). The Christian has also cleaved to Jesus. Prostitution has been attributed to sacred cult worship (associated with idolatry—in Corinth the goddess Aphrodite), but this may be unfounded.[6] However, prostitutes and *heterai* were not controlled by the law. This suggests that they were outside of the legal codes of appropriateness for both the civic and spiritual communities. This may be why Paul suggests that they destroy the spiritual body. The church was affected by this sin. A Christian who has sex outside of marriage damages the church, themselves, and the reputation of Christ in the community.

Another note should also be addressed. It seems that this sin was a major concern for Paul. He wrote that other sins are outside the body but this was the one that affected our own bodies (6:18). Sexual issues have provided major struggles for Christians, the church, and our communities. This is the area we have been hit the hardest. Ministers have been guilty of affairs and abusing their power sexually over other members. Adultery has brought shame on a church and destroyed families both inside and outside a congregation. Lawsuits for millions of dollars have been successfully passed for priests, clergy, and members who have mo-

---

6. Lanci, "The Stones Don't Speak," 220.

lested young boys and girls in the community. Sexual sin has damaged the name of Jesus in our culture. For Paul the sexual battle has been going for many millennia.

How does this affect us? We live in a world and a culture not unlike that in Paul's day. While sexual sin was rampant in the ancient Roman world, there were still moralists who cried out for moderation, respect, and self control. Today, sex is twisted by many in our world. Yet we also have moralists (Christian and non-Christian) who cry out for moderation, respect, and self control. Today sexual abuse is very common. Statistics indicate that one in five women will be raped by a male at least once in their lifetime. Internet pornography affects millions. One can open a new email account and within a month receive a constant stream of pornography web site invitations. Sexual abuse destroys victims as well as those who rape another human in the image of God. Pornography destroys men and reduces us to animals. It also enables an industry that tells women they should be treated as objects.

Sex outside of marriage destroys trust. It puts men and women at risk of being hurt and vulnerable. It is the easy way and the most destructive to our emotional system. It is part of the empire of power and affects all people in a church.

- The single man or woman who wants to be married but has not found someone or not compromised on their spiritual convictions to merely settle.
- The divorced man or woman who struggles for acceptance and tries to once again date in holiness and purity.
- The widow or widower who went from a healthy, loving, sexual relationship and is now single, grieving, and lonely.
- The young teen boy who hears from others that women are to be conquered and that manhood comes as it did in the Epic of Gilgamesh.
- The young teen girl who is coerced into sex because she is told that this will make him love her more.
- The countless men and women who struggle to know themselves because they were raped, molested, or used sexually by someone they knew.

- The men who struggle with sexual addiction because their first experience was as a young boy, it felt good, and they believe they are destined to this life of homosexuality.
- The young women who walk the streets as prostitutes who, because of years of abuse, have learned to disassociate from their bodies during sex and wonder if their will ever have a truly loving relationship. Their abusive pimps go untouched in the legal system because we blame the women for prostitution.

All of these people fight the same battle with Satan. All of these people struggle to know who they are. All of these people suffer. All of these people grieve. All of these people are exploited. All of these people want to be loved. All of these people are loved by God. All of these people can change. You are loved, you can change, and you deserve to have healthy relationships with others.

Paul hit the reset button in this section. For Paul the body can be in sync with the divine and honor God. While he wrote very boldly about sexual sin, something embraced by the Corinthian culture, he reminded them that they were loved by God. In this text he reminded them:

- "Some of you were like this, but you were washed (in baptism), you were made holy, you were justified in the name of the Lord Jesus Christ and by the Spirit of our (your) God."
- "Do you not know that your bodies are members of Christ?"
- "Don't you know that your body is a temple of the Holy Spirit, who is in you, whom you have received from God?"
- God loves you and has not abandoned you. God's Spirit lives within you and God has chosen you. You are still precious, even if you feel broken, and worth saving.

While some suggest that Paul addressed a third problem in the church, prostitution, I would like to suggest that this section provides a metaphor for the earlier problem. Just as Paul used the body as a metaphor for the church (3:19) Paul again suggested that the body was not meant for sexual sin. He used the word *porneia* eight times in 5:1–6:18 and began the section on marriage (7:1) concerning this word. For Paul sexual sin affected the community or body of Jesus. Not only that, it affected an individual's spiritual relationship to God.

Paul quoted a common statement for the Corinthians (6:12). "All things are lawful for me. . ." It seems that Roman culture expected young men to explore their manhood through irresponsible living such as drunkenness, sex with prostitutes, and wild partying. Over two thousand years little has changed. However, Paul suggests that this lifestyle and attitude was not beneficial for others. While the typical Roman male sought to indulge his body in sexual pleasures, Paul believed that this affected the body of Christ. Even more, Paul believed that this behavior affected those outside the body. Having sex with prostitutes continued to enslave these women in a life of evil, manipulation, and suffering. While the young man thought only of himself, Paul suggested that he think of his community, the prostitute, and those outside the body of Christ. His role was to bring honor to God, rather than shame.

Resetting the Button

Both chapters indicate that sexual sin is a selfish action. The man who had his father's woman and those who degraded their spiritual family in court were not operating as a body. They were destroying the body of Christ. They did this not only by sin, but by destroying the reputation of God in their community. Paul reminded them that they have a responsibility to others to build up, encourage, and strengthen.

Paul reminded them that they were still in Christ. First, *Paul mentioned that Jesus was still among them.* In chapter five, he talked about "presence" with a term used by the Roman Emperor for a presence in a city where he was not living. When Paul mentioned that he and Jesus were present he was reminding the church that they still had authority. By allowing evil to be among them the body was in danger of being infected. The individual was also at risk of destruction (1 Cor 3:17). The church needed to protect themselves and their reputations in their community.

Second, *Paul reminded them that they were a temple, a dwelling place for God. They were bought with a price.* In chapters three and six they were still God's field, building, temple, and body. Their sin, selfishness, and jealousy had not removed their name from the book of life, but they were dishonoring Jesus' name. They were shaming God both spiritually and publically. However, Paul reminded them that they were still owned by Jesus, and therefore were capable of more than what they were allowing to happen.

A MODEL FOR THE CHURCH

The church was not a place designed to judge the world. The church was not called to condemn others but to call them to repentance. The church is to be a place of transformation. God's mercy was always displayed in a willingness to send prophets to call people to repentance so that they could change, be healed, and bring glory to God. The church likewise is to go into the temporary empire and call people to a stable realm which is the empire of *agape*. In order for this to happen the church must have the following qualities.

First, *the church must be a safe place for all people*. Since the church at Corinth was predominantly poor, power was easy to abuse. Yet Paul wanted the church to be a place where men and women could empower each other, rather than destroy each other. Paul used the "reset" buttons to make sure that the community could cultivate trust, safety, and peace. In order for people to change, they must become vulnerable. Once they become vulnerable they must have a safe place to grow.

Second, *the church must be a place where power is shared, not abused*. This happens when we seek the benefit of others. Sexual power can be intoxicating and in the ancient world sexual power was used to humiliate others and define people's cultural standing. Homosexuality, prostitution, adultery, and sexual expressions may have been one person's attempt to explore their sexual freedom, however it cost many other's their dignity and honor in society. For Paul this was one reason that the world was "being abolished." The church was to be a place where people were strengthened, not destroyed. Since the church, unlike the world, was to be permanent and living it had to resist the behaviors that corrupted society and the culture.

Finally, *the church must provide guidance to people who live in a confused world*. The church was seen as the gateway to God's empire. Jesus' language about the kingdom/empire would have been viewed as politically incorrect. Paul referred to Jesus as "Lord Jesus" twenty-five times in 1 Cor 1–3. At Corinth Caesar was "Lord." However, Paul wanted the church to see themselves as part of a different empire. He wanted them to be an empire, temple, and community that guided people from confusion to peace.

> He wanted them to show others a better way.
> The way of *agape*.

4

Shared Sexual Power

MARRIAGE AND SEX

PAUL NEXT ADDRESSED QUESTIONS asked by the Corinthian Christians. He earlier mentioned that Chloe's slaves (Fortunatus and Achaicus) and Stephanus, have communicated with him concerning other issues (1 Cor 1:10; 16:17). It seems that they not only reported to Paul that the church was divided and formed human/leader allegiances (1:10), but may have shared that a man was sexual with his father's wife/concubine (5:1) and that they were divisive between poor and rich (11:17). Paul reminded them that he had also written a letter encouraging them to avoid those in the faith who were practicing these sinful lifestyles (5:9). Since Paul mentioned a previous letter, we think that 1 Corinthians was actually a second letter to the church. However, this letter may have been more in depth. It also seems that this was a response to their letter and questions.

Beginning with chapter seven they wanted to know about sexual relationships in marriage (7:1); if it was right to eat meat sacrificed to pagan gods (8:1); and about spirituality (12:1). Chapter seven continued Paul's thoughts concerning sexuality in the Corinthian culture and its affect on the people of Jesus. They asked the question, "Is it good for a man not to touch a woman?"

1 Cor 7:1–7

> Concerning what you wrote, "[that]It is good for a man not to touch [sexually] a woman." On account of inappropriate sexual behavior each [man] should have his own wife and each [woman] should have her own husband. The husband owes it [sex] to his wife, like-

wise the wife to her husband. The wife does not have authority over her own body, but the husband does. Likewise the husband does not have authority over his own body, but the wife does. Don't withhold from one another, except if you agree for a while to pursue study and prayer; but then come together again, so that Satan may not tempt you because of your lack of self-control. This is my suggestion, not a command. I wish that all were like me but each has their own gift from God, one of one kind and one of another.

There have been many suggestions concerning the background and interpretations of this text. Some suggest that Paul was critical of those who married, stating that they were weak because they could not exercise self control. Others may suggest that Paul was writing in response to strict Jewish and Greek movements which prohibited sexual contact even in marriage. These movements suggested that abstinence made men more spiritual. Others believed that Paul was critiquing the Roman culture which compelled men to marry rather than stay single. This "state marriage" created a relationship out of compulsion rather than love. Understanding the history of the culture will be helpful in applying Paul's message to the church both at Corinth and today.

In the early part of his reign Caesar Augustus became alarmed at what he saw was the corruption and digression of the Roman family and Roman state.[1] He enacted tax breaks for Roman citizens who were married and had children. Single citizens and couples without children experienced a sense of rejection in these reforms. Augustus also punished men and women for adultery. Due to this legislation, many Roman men married young women/girls who kept house and raised their families. The Roman men had sexual relationships outside the home and expected the wives to be sexually pure. Many marriages existed in name only. For the men love, sexual sharing, and romance existed outside the home. For the women it rarely existed.

The Epicurean and Stoic philosophers reacted to the sexual immorality of their culture by suggesting that sexual intercourse was bad for the body and a person's leisure time.[2] Sexual intercourse was also something to be resisted since it made a person unholy, weak, or unclean. Jeffers indicated that a Roman graffiti has been found stating, "baths, wine and love-making destroy our bodies, yet love-making, wine and baths make

1. Winter, *Roman Wives*, 39–47.
2. Ward, "Musonius and Paul on Marriage," 284–88.

life worth living."³ In marriage, a spouse was praised for abstinence, even at the expense of their partner. On the surface, Paul's statement, "It is good for a man not to have sexual relations with a woman," seems to suggest that Paul was telling the church that sex was bad. However, Paul many times quoted the Corinthian's opinions rather than his own.

> "Everything is permissible . . ." (1 Cor 6:12)
> "Food is for the stomach . . ." (1 Cor 6:13)
> "It is good for a man not to have sexual relations with a woman . . ." (1 Cor 7:1)
> "Let's eat, drink, and be merry, because we may die tomorrow . . ." (1 Cor 15:32)

Paul and Sexual Relations

Paul began this section by stating their opinion, not his own (7:1). Many of Paul's teachings are similar to the Stoic philosophers such as:[4]

- The apostles as public spectacle (4:9)
- Argument from conscience (8:7)
- Value in being free and living without attachments (7:29–32; 9:1,19)
- Body imagery and the Spirit working in harmony with the body (12)
- Imitating God
- Self sufficiency

While some of Paul's teachings were similar to the Stoics, concerning the issue of marriage, sex, and fulfillment he was much different. The Corinthians were the ones asking if sex with a woman was bad, not Paul. "Concerning the matters about which you wrote, [that] 'It is good for a man not to have sexual relations with a woman.'" Throughout the text Paul acknowledged that sex was good. He also admitted that it was a strong temptation to men and women. The common teaching in Corinth was that this passion was unhealthy and needed to be curbed. Another view suggested that sexual pleasure, for men, was to be enjoyed by prostitutes or *heterai*, not one's wife. However, this idea did not come from Paul but

---

3. Jeffers, 29.
4. Terence Paige, "Stoicism," 209–15.

popular philosophers and teachers.⁵ Paul suggested that sexual relationships were good and meant to be shared in marriage. First, he mentioned that marriage was an opportunity to satisfy a desire that *both men and women* had for sexual intimacy. In chapters five and six Paul discussed how dangerous sex had become in their culture and that the church was to be a place of transformation. Here he provided an opportunity for men and women to express their God given sexuality in the relationship of marriage.

Second, Paul mentioned that the each spouse owns their partner's body. For Paul, marriage was not a one sided relationship. Men and women had the opportunity to sexually *satisfy their partner*. While most Roman men believed that they controlled every aspect of their families (especially their wives), Paul wrote that Roman men were also submissive to their wives' sexual needs. Contrary to what the current philosophers were writing about abstinence and spirituality, Paul encouraged couples to be concerned with their partner's sexual needs and desires. Sex was not only to be enjoyed by the individual; it was to be enjoyed by the partner.

Third, Paul acknowledged that *once a couple was married, they would continue to have sexual needs*. Paul allowed for separation for a period of leisure or reflection, but strongly urged that this be the desire of "both" individuals and that it be temporary.⁶ The word for agreement is the word leisure. Some Roman writers felt that sex encroached upon one's leisure activities. Paul seems to be accommodating those who strongly hold this view. However, their personal convictions should not override their partner's emotional and sexual needs. Satan would attack their sexual needs and weaknesses which would cause one partner to struggle. Paul believed that both husband and wife needed to please each other. The fact that Paul included the wives in this concession illustrates how radical Christianity was in the male dominated culture of ancient Corinth. Musonius Rufus, the Roman Stoic, suggested that sex was not to provide enjoyment in a marriage.

> Men who are not wantons or immoral are bound to consider sexual intercourse justified only when it occurs in marriage and is indulged in for the purpose of begetting children. Since that is

5. Ibid.

6. Roman philosophers suggested that sexual intercourse destroyed leisure time. Paul gave concession to those who wish to abstain from sex for this leisure time. This, however, was to be only a brief period and one after mutual consent. Ibid.

lawful, but unjust and unlawful when it is mere pleasure – seeking even in marriage.[7]

Finally Paul admitted that while abstinence was a gift, it was not for everyone. As he does so often in his call to discipleship, Paul compared himself with the ancient philosophers who used their strict lifestyle as a model for others. He was also celibate. However, Paul acknowledged that not everyone could be like him. His was a gift, not an example or type for others to follow, unless they felt called to that situation. It is incredible that Paul, as a single—celibate leader, still encouraged sex to be shared within a marriage.

Paul's comments on sexual intimacy in marriage were counter-cultural for his time. It seems odd to those of us in the twenty-first century that loveless marriages could exist but with the rise in divorce in both the US and Christian churches, we understand that many marriages experience dysfunction. The emphasis that many Christian family organizations have placed upon healthy marriages suggests that many religious families are in crises. One issue that I find common, as a minister and team leader with the Association of Marriage and Family Ministries, concerns sexual intimacy. I have met many trainers within this organization whose focus has been to help couples restore sexual intimacy in their marriages.

Many couples experience periods of sexual abstinence in their marriages due to health, disabilities, past traumatic experiences, depression, erectile dysfunction, and other issues. This presents a problem and may require one partner to sacrifice their sexual needs for the other. However, *both couples should work together to restore intimacy*. This requires working with their physician, counselor, therapist, or other health professional. The church must also minister to both partners and guide them to intimacy. This may be difficult but marriage is teamwork and one partner should not control the other's sexual needs. The work will also provide the emotional support needed for the couple.

Living in a mobile society has caused many couples to experience separation for lengthy periods of time. Those in the military may be deployed for months or years. While this is unavoidable the church should emphasize to governments that they are putting many families at risk. It seems odd that a country so concerned about family values does not understand that being at war can contribute to divorce, infidelity,

---

7. Musonius Rufus, trans. Cora Lutz, 86.

prostitution, and pornographic addictions. While I support our military troops, abuse is six times greater in military families than civilian.[8] Pornography, soldier rape, prostitution, and adultery have become common in the armed forces. The media continues to illustrate the struggles that military families face with an absent parent/spouse, especially those participating in multiple tours of duty. In the Association of Marriage and Family Ministries our discussions have also involved military chaplains who indicate that military families are at tremendous risk, especially now that thousands are deployed to the Middle East. While we are told that they are protecting our country, freedom, and the oppressed, we wonder who is protecting their families who also make the ultimate sacrifice. The church, also called to protect and empower families, like the prophets must hold our government accountable as well.

Finally, our mobile society also encourages employees to travel for extended periods of time. Those whose jobs require them to be apart from their spouses should consult with their partners. It is not fair to ask one's spouse to sacrifice their sexual needs for extended periods of time due to an occupation. It is not healthy to put oneself in sexual temptation because of a job. I have had to counsel men who travel often as truck drivers, regional salesmen, coaches, or other occupations through an affair. They also are not aware that their spouse was equally tempted. They did not realize that "I have to work to pay for this family," is not an acceptable excuse.

Bottom line, it is only a job—God will always provide. However, you can't always get another spouse, children, or family. If your boss works in the empire of power they will resist you. If they work in the empire of *agape* or even understand that reality, they will support you. Even more, Jesus will bless you.

Single for Jesus

1 Cor 7:8–9

> To those who are not married, and the widows,
> its good for them to stay like me [single]
> If they cannot practice self-control, they should marry,
> its better to marry than to be aflame with passion.

---

8. Clark, *Setting the Captives Free*, 47.

For those who, like Paul, were unmarried Paul recommended that they could stay single. This was a stark contrast to common Roman policy but Paul believed that single Christians had a place in the kingdom. They also had a valuable role in both leadership and ministry. Paul believed that they could continue in their state which God had called them (7:17, 20, 22, 24). Some in the church, who were slaves, may have been resigned to a life of being unmarried and celibate. Some, as slaves, would have been prostitutes, pimps, sex slaves, *hetaerae*, eunuchs, or horribly mutilated and traumatized physically and sexually. For them, being single would not have been a problem. Paul suggested that they remain as they were. The church was a family that accepted them for who they were. Even if they had become free, they did not need to return to a life of slavery.

Those who were single did not need to feel compelled to follow Roman policy. While the government may have discriminated against them they had the opportunity to focus completely on serving Jesus (7:28, 32, 35). Paul mentioned that the world was passing away suggesting that the empire that affected their lives was powerless (7:31). Corinth experienced many earthquakes during the mid first century as well as three or four major famines. For Paul, the single Christian had an opportunity to survive these crises and persecution without concern for a family.

Those who were single and engaged also had the opportunity to continue as single individuals. Paul gave them permission to release their fiancé (7:36–38) without being penalized. For Paul, if they chose to marry, it was not a sin. If they chose to leave their fiancé and remain single, they were in a better position.

1 Cor 7:36–38

> If someone thinks they are acting dishonorably toward their virgin
>   [fiancé]
> if his passions are strong,
> let him do as he wishes, they should marry.
>
> It is not a sin.
>
> But whoever is firmly established in his heart,
> not compelled but having his desire under control,
> and has determined this in his heart,
> to keep her as his betrothed, he will do well.
>
> The one who marries his betrothed does well,
> and he who refrains from marriage will do even better.

Single women who were widows also had permission to stay unmarried (7:39). Paul encouraged them to marry a Christian. However, Paul continued to give single men and women permission to stay as they were, and serve Jesus in ministry. In a world that was difficult for single men and women, Christianity embraced and empowered them to ministry.

To the Married

1 Cor 7:10–16

> To those married I give this command
> (not I, but the Lord)
> the wife should not separate from her husband
> (but if she does, she should remain unmarried or else be reconciled to her husband),
> and the husband should not divorce his wife.
>
> To the rest I say
> (I, not the Lord)
> that if any brother has a wife who is an unbeliever, and she agrees to stay with him, he should not divorce her.
> If any woman has a husband who is an unbeliever, and he agrees to stay with her, she should not divorce him.
>
> Because the unbelieving husband is made holy because of his wife, and the unbelieving wife is made holy because of her husband. Otherwise your children would be unclean, instead they are holy.
>
> However, if the unbelieving partner separates,
> let them go.
> In such cases the brother or sister is not enslaved.
> God has called you to peace.
>
> Wife, how do you know whether you will save your husband?
> Husband, how do you know whether you will save your wife?

Paul also addressed those who were married. In a world that encouraged the institution of marriage but spoke down to sexual fulfillment in marriage Paul wrote that this was an enjoyable relationship. He gave the command that a couple should not separate or divorce. If they separated, they were to reconcile. Paul mentioned that Jesus had spoken this command (7:10) which would refer to his comments in the Gospels (Matt 19:1–12; Mark 10:1–12; Luke 16:18). In the Gospels Jesus spoke against the Jewish rabbis who looked for reasons to divorce their wives. In the *Mishnah* (a collection of Jewish rabbinical teachings in which many were popular during Jesus' time) the chapter *Gittin* is filled with reasons for divorce. The tract also suggested many valid methods to ending a marriage. During the time of Jesus, and even into this century, marriage was/is an institution that enslaved women. According to Jesus men needed to stop looking for reasons to divorce their wives and should develop the relationship that God had given them. Paul suggested that Jesus had already spoken on the issue, "I give this command (not I but the Lord) . . ." Paul reinforced Jesus' teaching by calling couples to reconcile and stay together.

In the Roman Empire women were able to divorce but had a difficult time. Men, however, could dismiss their wives simply by saying, "Get your things and go . . ." or "I release you . . ." In light of the *Mishnah* it seems that the Jews imitated this process in their treatment of women. Paul suggested that this was not the way for Christian couples. Christian couples were to work to build a healthy marriage and seek reasons to stay together. Christian couples express a counter-cultural view of marriage by both parties working together.

Paul next spoke to another group, the mixed marriages. "To the rest I say, not the Lord . . ." This suggests two points. First, Jesus had not spoken on this issue. Whatever group Paul addressed he acknowledged that it was a group not addressed in the Gospels. Paul, however, did have authority to speak to this group. Here Paul exercised his right as an apostle. While Jesus' statements on marriage addressed the Jewish community Paul believed that it applied to those also who were within the faith community. However, many spouses were converted to Jesus without their partners. This presented the church with a problem. Paul suggested that Jesus' sayings, in the Gospels, did not apply to these "mixed marriages."

Mixed marriages were a concern for the church. One common story in the early church described how a married woman was converted to Christianity. Her husband was very immoral with prostitution, drunkenness, and idolatry. His wife challenged him to come to Jesus but to no avail. The husband had her thrown into jail for being a Christian and divorced her. She was later martyred while her husband was overcome with sorrow for having her persecuted.[9] This story illustrates the issues some Christians faced in mixed marriages.

---

9. Justin, *2 Apology*, 2.

The group of people which Paul addressed was Christians married to "unbelievers." While the word used for the unbeliever (*apistos*) was used by ancient philosophers for an unreliable, untrustworthy, or bad man, Paul did not treat this individual the same way. He encouraged the Christian to continue in the marriage if the unbeliever was willing to stay. A Christian who was married to one who did not follow Jesus had two options. They could encourage the unbeliever to see Jesus through love, compassion, and justice; or they could be pulled into idolatry, sexual sin, or other moral struggles. Historically, many Christian spouses were persecuted by their unbelieving partners. In many cases Christians had to divorce their unbelieving spouse. This was because these Christians took an aggressive stance to their marriage. The Christian was called to stand for their faith, promote peace in their home, and sanctify their spouse. Christians were not called to passively endure sin and abuse in their families. They were called to transform their homes and their communities. Christian spouses had an opportunity to lead their unbelieving spouse into the way of *agape*. In many cases the partner was willing to stay and experience the love that God had for all people.

According to Paul, in 1 Cor 7:12–16, the Christian should accept the unbelieving spouse if they wished to stay in the marriage. It was likely that the Christian spouse would expect Jesus to reign over the home rather than become passive to the other spouse's immoral behavior. However, if the unbelieving spouse did not wish to stay, Paul used the imperative in his statement, "let them go," or "send them away." This imperative language was used by Roman men to legally divorce their wives but here Paul gave permission for the Christian spouse to do the same. Male or female had permission to say, "Go!"

Too often Christians become victims in a marriage. The church's strict stance against divorce seems to be stronger than God's stance. We have responded to the rise in divorce by forbidding it. In doing this we have, in my opinion, done the following:

- Continued the increase of divorce in the faith community.
- Given abuse victims little, if any, way out of an abusive marriage.
- Emotionally kept men and women in marriages where their spouse continues with dysfunctional behavior such as drugs, alcohol, pornography, violent mental illness, pedophilia, and other behaviors that destroy family peace.

- Made these spouses victims in the marriage.
- Contributed to the emotional damage of the children who are exposed to these unhealthy models in their parents.
- Not empowered the Christian spouse to seek their own emotional and intimate well-being. They have not been able to take a stand for Jesus and confront the dysfunction.
- Taught the children that marriage is an institution in need of preservation rather than a relationship that nurtures people.
- Propagated the myth that by submission all Christians will turn their spouse to Jesus when the majority of these Christian spouses have been oppressed and their children exposed to dysfunctional behavior.
- Brought guilt and shame upon divorced Christians.
- Indirectly led to the rise in young people both leaving the church and an increase in cohabitation.

I was presenting at a domestic violence training for clergy at a church in Eugene, Oregon. One of the rabbis attending came to me and wanted to share his take on the evangelical community and its lack of response to addressing domestic abuse. While acknowledging that the Jewish community had its own struggles to help victims he mentioned that the evangelical church took a strong stance against divorce, which does not empower the victim to leave. I agreed and shared with him how difficult it has been to get clergy to even admit that abuse can violate the marriage covenant.[10] He replied, "But you all are looking at it from the marriage and its permanence standpoint. We believe in *Shalom Bayit* (peace in the home) and for us violence destroys peace in the home." He was right. In fact when he mentioned this I thought of Paul's statement in 1 Cor 7:16, "God has called us to peace."

Paul indicated, in this section, that marriage was not only about fulfilling each other's sexual needs; it involved fulfilling each other's emotional needs. Marriage was never designed to enslave people; it is a place of safety, security, empowerment, and support. When Jesus confronted

---

10. While I understand that this opens a larger discussion concerning Jesus' statements in the Gospels concerning fornication as "the only reason for divorce," Paul does allow divorce for other issues. For a deeper discussion of this see: Clark, *Setting the Captives Free*, 143–80; David Instone-Brewer, *Marriage and Divorce in the Bible*.

the religious leaders of his day concerning divorce (Matt 19; Mark 10) he was addressing a group of leaders who had made it difficult for women to find security in their marriage. Even today, many women are emotional and physical prisoners in their homes because their husbands claim to have divine authority over them.

However, God has empowered women and children to be safe from these forms of abuse and discouragement. Divorce is an aggressive attempt to protect the sanctity and honor of the marital relationship. Divorce confronts dysfunction in a marriage and allows the offended spouse to seek peace, safety, and emotional security. God practiced this divorce by opposing dysfunction in the covenant relationship with Israel. In Jeremiah 3:8 God gave a certificate of divorce to a nation that abused God and dishonored the covenant. Likewise if we empower Christian spouses to confront dysfunction in this way we will:

- See confrontation that can lead to healing
- Help the dysfunctional spouse obtain help to be the kind of person God called them to be
- Teach children that marriage is to be a healthy relationship that addresses dysfunction
- Promote marriage as a two way street

Paul taught that Christians had the right to expect godly behavior in their homes. While this does not mean that the unbeliever has to change it does suggest that the couple can have a healthy, loving, monogamous relationship without conversion. The children can live in a peaceful home. The Christian does not "take advantage" or "disrespect" their partner but honors them for their love in the relationship.

I have met many unbelieving spouses who are good, loving, committed partners and parents. They are not convinced that Jesus is Lord, but they do provide what Paul saw as a necessary ingredient to a healthy marriage. The church can be more effective strengthening the couple's relationship and respecting the unbelieving spouse. This unconditional love reflects God's glory and helps the unbelieving spouse feel supported rather than suspected by the church. Through time many are led to Jesus because they see the church as a family and a place of transformation.

I have met "believing" spouses who were immoral and abusive. Believing is not confined to a confession but a lifestyle, a practice, a belief system. In some cases this "unbelieving" spouse is also a hindrance to their Christian partner. They also are not good parents and place the family at risk. Paul gives the Christian the opportunity to send them away. This was a divorce by Roman standards as well. Christians are not bound to stay in a relationship that destroys their faith, spirit, and self-esteem. They also should protect their children. For Paul the children must live in a peaceful home. Paul also does not forbid the Christian from remarrying, as he does with those divorcing from a Christian spouse. Therefore, the church should not bind them where they have been set free.

Slaves in the Empire

Paul next discussed slavery. In the ancient world some sold themselves into slavery to pay off their debts. Others sold family members. Other slaves were conquered in battle. Some could work their way out of slavery financially through a *peculium*. Slavery was not always a place of pain and suffering. Slavery was many times a convenient lifestyle for one in debt to provide for themselves and have a job.[11] However, slavery did put people in a position of humiliation, oppression, and vulnerability. Other's sold themselves into slavery to receive status and honor.[12] Paul's analogy to slavery suggested that the Corinthian Christians did not need to enter any relationship which became a form of slavery. While slavery was not always bad in the ancient world, Paul suggested that people not put themselves in this position. However, Paul wanted the members of Christ's body to remember that Jesus owned them.

> "You were bought at a price, do not become slaves of men/humans . . ."

Paul wanted the Corinthians to be free from oppression both in and out of the church. This applied to marriage, slavery, and sexual relationships.

Paul's words are important for us today.

First, *the church must proclaim healing, love, grace, mercy, and sexual fulfillment in marriages.* Rather than "keeping marriages together," we must encourage marriages to be vibrant relationships of love, fulfillment, and peace. Rather than suggesting that men and women lose their identity

---

11. Witherington, *Conflict and Community in Corinth*, 181–85.
12. Judge, 147–48.

or become enslaved to an institution we must teach them that marriage completes and complements.

Second, *the church must empower women in relationships.* In Gen 2:18 the woman was a helper suitable for the man. The Hebrew word was *neged* which meant opposite, south, or complement. Women and men complement each other in marriage. Women are not inferior to men, they are partners in marriage. For this reason Paul showed concern in how women were viewed in the church and their surrounding community. For Paul they had rights in marriage. They could allow their immoral husbands, who did not honor the marriage covenant or their Christian faith, to leave the marriage. He also acknowledged that the apostle's wives were partners with their husband's ministry (1Cor 9:5). They were not to be used and oppressed sexually in prostitution, sexual abuse, or other controlling relationships. They could prophesy (1 Cor 11). They were to have their heads covered and be silent in the assembly (1 Cor 11, 14). This was a way of protecting them. Only prostitutes and courtesans were allowed in the presence of males during a meal/gathering. Paul showed concern for their reputations. Paul respected women and, unlike many in the Roman Empire, sought to empower and protect their reputation. Even more, he sought to empower women to practice ministry.

Paul also sought to empower singles. In the US our churches are filled with singles and single parents. Singles (divorced, individual, or never married) represent a significant percentage of our churches and population. Many have shared with me that they feel alone and pressure to be in a romantic relationship. Even more, many feel invalidated for their reasons to not marry, date, or remarry.

After a final edit to this chapter I met with the director for a local prostitution alternatives organization whom we work with in our ministry. She was asking about the manuscript and I told her about Paul's emphasis to the Corinthians (some who may have been former sex slaves) concerning being single in a culture that penalized them for not choosing to marry. The director smiled, nodded her head, and began to share about some of the men and women who have been in their program. These men and women are asked to be celibate while they are in the program. Her opinion is that they need to recover their childhood and sexual innocence. Those who are celibate for two to three years tend to heal and recover from the pain of sexual abuse and prostitution. Most have been introduced to sex with an adult as children and need to find that innocence.

Then she slowed down in her speech and said, "Most of them have no desire to ever marry or have sexual relationships. They are comfortable just being who they are. However, they still need community, friends, and support." As I left our meeting it hit me. What an opportunity for the church to support and encourage those who have no desire for marriage. How lonely they must be in a *oikoumenē* which pushes them to marry or be sexually involved with someone. How lonely they must be in a church that targets marriages, families, and couples. How liberating it must be to hear that they have a gift, a purpose, and an opportunity to serve God with undivided devotion. I hope we have the chance to share that message with them.

Some people desire to focus on their careers. Others wish to focus on raising and enjoying their children. Some have been traumatized sexually and feel no desire for a romantic relationship with the opposite sex. Others feel that their past relationship was sufficient and satisfying enough that they do not desire another. Some struggle with their sexual orientation due to a traumatic past and wish to remain single. Whatever the reason—Paul called it a gift and said that there was no shame in being single.

Unlike the empire of power the church must accept and empower singles to feel supported, useful, and comfortable to "stay in the state in which they were called." Singles have a tremendous ministry for Jesus. They can encourage teens and young singles who struggle with sexual purity. They can devote more time to ministry and serving Jesus. They should not be seen as a sexual temptation for others, but powerful tools for the kingdom. At Agape I have witnessed not only the spiritual maturity manifested by many singles—but the drive and commitment they bring to the church. I have also listened to the pain and loneliness they feel while living in a culture that pressures sexual relationships and makes them feel empty or incomplete.

When I first started ministry I was helping a church in a small Missouri town. I had helped an older chaplain at the state rehabilitation school with his mid week services. I became familiar with many of the mentally and physically handicapped kids at the school. Two of the young boys/men would accompany me to church. I was single at the time and would talk to the young boys about being appropriate with the women at church. I also knew that some of the female staff at the school would sexually tease the young boys while on duty. I shared with them that they needed to avoid these women, not because of the sexual temptation, but because I felt that they were humiliating the boys.

The director of the school called me to his office one day. He knew my father, who had been a psychologist at the school years before, and we had a good visit. He mentioned to me that some of the female staff suggested I was homosexual and that I might be pushing that on the boys. I explained what I had told the boys and why I was suggesting they avoid these women. He nodded in agreement and mentioned that it was a problem at the school. He also asked, "Why would someone think that you were gay, even thought you went to church?" I responded, "Probably because we live in a world that expects us to act out our desires sexually. Many people also feel that if men are trying to be sexually pure then there is something wrong with them." He agreed because he too attended church.

While I struggled with lust and sexual purity as a young man and admit to failing at times, I know that during my early years as a Christian the thought of choosing to be abstinent has been strange in an empire of power—as it was centuries ago. However, Jesus calls us, especially men, to be proactive in our purity while single, even if this is a counter-cultural message.

Third, *we need reset buttons for those who have been slaves to sexual, traumatic, and abusive forms of power.* Paul reminds Christians that while they are free they are servants of Jesus. As servants they live in an empire that is permanent, peaceful, and empowering in marriage. All relationships in which Christians enter are meant to bring joy, peace, and love. This is a reflection of the relationship Jesus has with them. While we see a fading empire of lust, power, rejection, and even sexual abuse and neglect, Paul warns us not to embrace that empire. The church has the opportunity to cultivate and model relationships that bless all people. While Rome forced its citizens into a mold, the empire of Jesus accepted all people and provided a place for transformation. It also gave them leaders who took ownership of the people and guided them to healing, joy, and a feeling of value.

JESUS: A MODEL FOR THE EMPIRE OF AGAPE

As the initiator of a new covenant relationship Jesus serves as a model for marriage. Marriages, like the covenant with Jesus, are relationships which are to bring peace, healing, love, hope, safety, and empowerment. In the church these relationships should bring glory to God and be attractive to those outside the empire of *agape*. Divorce happens when these relationships fail to provide support and nurturing to *both partners*. Relationships are never mean to enslave others, they are meant to empower.

The same is true of all relationships that God's people enter. In the Roman Empire relationships were many times used to oppress, manipulate, and control others for the betterment of the powerful. Christians, however, are to seek relationships that help them mature, develop, feel loved and supported, and grow closer to God. These types of relationships also help those who do not name Jesus as Lord grow and develop. The church can become a safe place for Christians and non-Christians by encouraging its members to practice *agape*. The church can also go into the world to create sacred spaces and sacred relationships through love which help outsiders see Jesus as one who initiates relationship rather than as one who uses relationship to oppress others.

> The better way expresses better relationships.
> The better way expresses *agape* in relationships.

5

Empowering Others

LET THE GAMES BEGIN!

CORINTH WAS A CITY which had a public official in charge of their sporting events, especially the Isthmian Games. His official title was *Agonothete*. His main job was to make sure that these games were financially supported and that athletes competed according to the rules. Historians who have studied the list of champions from the various sporting events in the Roman Empire have suggested that Asia Minor was producing more champions than Greece in these games.[1] Greece, the originator of these games, needed to "beef up" their sporting events to provide more champions. The *Agonothete* may have been someone who was hired to make sure this happened.

While Corinth lay in ruins the nearby city of Sicyon took responsibility for the Isthmian Games. After Corinth was rebuilt Augustus returned the games to the city around 40 CE.[2] The Roman colony had a vested interest in hosting these games, as well as the Roman Caesarean games, held in the off years of the Isthmian contests. Corinthian civic pride was associated with these games which also became a vehicle to continue the spread of Greek history, culture, and identity in the Roman colony. The Isthmian games were not just contests, they were a civic and social identity for the Corinthians. During the Roman Imperial period there were two-hundred-seventy professional athletic festivals in the Greco-Roman world.[3]

---

1. Scanlon, 58–65.

2. Gebhard, "Rites for Melikertes," 183, 185–86; Clarke, *Secular and Christian Leadership*, 17.

3. Scanlon, 29.

The *Agonothete* was a wealthy individual and ruler (male or female) who was elected to this position. Their role was to financially fund the games. While their own personal finances would have been necessary, they also had the opportunity to solicit funds from other elite citizens in the area. This would have been done through dinner parties, banquets, and individual invites to a meal.[4] Since Poseidon was the god of these games, sacrifices would have been offered to him. Those who were wealthy would be invited to the dinner. Those who were wannabees sought this honor as well. The poor would rarely be invited to a dinner with any thought of soliciting funds. However, Corinthian Christians such as Gaius, Sosthenese, Chloe, Phoebe, and Erastus may have been invited to attend these dinners and support the games.[5] These dinners were also viewed as spiritual events.

Inside Corinth were various places for sporting events. Starting gates for a short sprint course have been found in the *agora* near the *Agonothete's* office. A crude stadium for races also existed inside the city walls. It seems that the citizens in Corinth were able to view races outside of the Isthmian stadium, possibly places for future athletes to test their athletic skills.

Archaeologists have uncovered altar stands in the dining rooms of ancient homes. The walls also contain paintings of the various deities worshipped by the homeowner. Many contained murals of Hestia (goddess of the hearth) and the Laurels. Statues of gods were also present at the meal. In the ancient world the meal was viewed as a spiritual experience. Both Dionysius and Zeus were usually praised when the cup of wine was passed at each meal.[6] There was also a small temple that offered food to those attending the theater in Corinth.[7] This would also have offered cultic food to theatergoers. Eating in Corinth was a spiritual event.

Sharing meals has always been a spiritual experience. I have noticed that when I give money to those spanging it is less personal than taking the man or woman to eat something. Sometimes we go under one of the many bridges in Portland to take one seeking shelter for a meal. As we sit and converse we "break bread together" (or even better a Big Mac or a Chipotle burrito) and invite each other into our lives. When I share that I

4. Winter, *After Paul Left Corinth*, 5.
5. It is even possible that Erastus, as an official, at one time may have been appointed to fulfill the role of *agonothete*.
6. Smith, 29.
7. Williams, 223.

am a minister doing this for no motives but to meet them, the conversation always turns to a discussion about God. Some of the young boys I invite find it a relief. Portland's nickname is "boy's town" because many pedophiles solicit sex from the male street kids in exchange for money, food, or drugs. This puts these kids on edge. After a lengthy discussion over lunch they finally relax and enjoy the conversation. However, during this meal, we are experiencing what men and women have experienced for years. Sharing food, conversation, and our hearts has a deeply spiritual implication for humans. It is a time when we give thanks for each other and the food that we are given. Eating with those who are homeless has an even more spiritual element to it. We become vulnerable and realize that God gives all things to us graciously and unselfishly. For a brief moment I learn what it is like to be homeless and in need.

In the ancient world meals typically involved sacrifices and invocations to the gods, especially the one closest to the host. In the case of the *Agonothete*, Poseidon would most likely have been the god of preference since the Isthmian Games were held near his temple in Isthmia. At Corinth dining halls have been uncovered in the temple of Asklepius, the god of healing. Apollo would also have had a strong presence at meals. Older temples for Demeter also contain dining halls, but this may have been before Corinth was destroyed by the Romans. Hestia, the goddess of the hearth, and the Laurels were also deities invoked during meals. Many times when meat was served it was assumed that a sacrifice had been given to a god. During Paul's time Corinth had expanded their meat market which would have had a large supply of sacrificial meat. If the meat was bought in the market the merchant may have made the distinction between sacred meat and normal meat. Whatever the condition, wealthy individuals were constantly placed in the presence of idols, gods, goddesses, and sacred dinners. Eating was considered a spiritual event.

Eating Meat at Fundraising Dinners

1 Cor 8:1–13

    Concerning idolatry—we understand that we know a lot.

        Knowledge puffs up

        Love builds up

> If someone thinks that they might know better, they do not know as they should
>
> If someone loves God, they are known by him.
>
> Concerning food offered to idols
>> We know that there are many idols in the world and that there is one God even though there are many gods, whether in heaven or earth.
>>
>> But for us there is one God, the father over all and we are in him
>>
>> One Lord Jesus Christ, all things are his and so are we.
>
> Not everyone knows this.
> Some have the habit of eating food offered to idols in an idol's temple but because their conscience is vulnerable they become unclean.
>
> Food doesn't present us to God, whether or not we eat it doesn't make us better. Be aware that this right you have doesn't become a problem for those who are vulnerable. If someone, whose conscience is vulnerable, sees you, "the strong one," reclining [in a dining room with others] in [the presence] of an idol wont they be encouraged to eat food sacrificed to idols.
>
> With your knowledge you destroyed a vulnerable brother/sister, Christ died for them.
> You sinned against your brother/sister by bruising their weak conscience.
> You sin against Christ.
>
> If food offends my brother and sister, I won't eat meat in this realm so that I don't offend them.

Paul's concern in this text was not about the wealthy Christian who realized that Jesus was Lord and believed that there was no other gods. They were strong in their faith, or at least they claimed to be. Paul's concern was for those who were struggling with letting go of other gods. His concern was for those struggling with the Roman Empire's claim to be a powerful deity. His concern was for the converted Jews who came from a history of people punished by God for flirting with idolatry and the sexual issues that accompanied it (1 Cor 10:1–12). His concern was for those in the church who looked up to the leaders (and maybe formed alliances) and assumed that they continued their practice of polytheism. I used the term "vulnerable" for the Greek word "weak" because I believe it represents the issues of power and trust that Paul addressed in Corinth.

Polytheism involved fear, control, and manipulation. Abandoning polytheism did not just involve "thinking differently" but addressing the sense of fear, paranoia, and loss of control over natural phenomena. It also meant leaving one's family and associations. Many who left polytheism had to overcome their fears from curses (placed on them from family and friends), being scapegoats for natural disasters, and letting go of years of teaching from loved ones. While religion at Corinth was undergoing tremendous transition, there were those who had no fear of the pagan deities that dotted the city's landscape.[8] Paul seemed afraid that these "strong Christians" had forgotten how to care for those they considered "weak." Paul was also concerned that those who thought that they were strong were not acting out of love.

Some of the Corinthians were exercising this freedom through their advanced knowledge. These Christians would have been educated and understood that the fear of gods, demons, and spiritual powers may have belonged to the lower class, uneducated, and superstitious. They may also have felt that the Jews were too traditional and controlled by fear. However, Paul, while accepting that idolatry was nothing, admitted that those who were vulnerable needed to be heard and respected.

The Corinthians requested Paul's opinion on this issue as is evident by his statement, "Now concerning food offered to idols . . ." This would have been a question asked by those who may have attended one of the a\ *Agonothete* feasts or been present at a dinner where a god was involved. Those asking the question may have been defending their behavior in a contested issue in the church. Traditionally the Jewish Christians would have felt very strongly about associating with idolatry not only from a personal conviction, but also as it would have affected their relationships with Corinthian Jews in their families and community. Since Sosthenes was part of Paul's team, he would have had much to say about life as a Jew in Corinth. He and Paul would have felt strongly about this side of the issue as was clear by their discussion about the Jewish history and idolatry. In this context it is easy to see that friction would have existed between the "strong" and "vulnerable" in the church.

---

8. Walbank, 278; Williams, 246.

An Example from Jewish History

1 Cor 10:1–13

> I don't want you to be uninformed brothers and sisters concerning our fathers (relatives) who
>> were all under the cloud,
>> and all passed through the sea,
>> and all were baptized into Moses (by the cloud and by the sea),
>> and all ate the same spiritual food,
>> and all drank the same spiritual drink.
>
> For they drank from the spiritual rock that followed/accompanied them
>> the rock was Christ.
>
> God was not pleased with many of them and they were scattered in the wilderness.
>
> These things took place for our example, so that we might not desire evil like them.
>
> Do not
>> be idolaters like some of them; as it is written,
>>> "The people sat down to eat and drink and rose up to play."
>> practice sexual immorality as some of them did,
>>> and twenty-three thousand fell in a single day.
>> test Christ, as some of them did
>>> and were destroyed by snakes,
>> grumble, as some of them did
>>> and were destroyed by the Destroyer.
>
> Now these things happened to them for our example,
>> but they have been written to warn us,
>>> the ones who have arrived at the realm of maturity.
>
> If you think you stand [are strong] watch out that you don't fall [sin].

Paul's comments above suggest that those who took idolatry lightly lacked the understanding of how it had damaged generations of people historically. Idolatry was not only worshipping statues and images of gods, but involved sexual immorality (as mentioned earlier in this book), prostitution, human sacrifice, and rebellion from God. In reading the history of the Jewish nation God constantly struggled with them as they turned from the covenant and degraded themselves with foreign gods. In 750 BCE and 600 BCE the Israelites and Jews were finally destroyed and taken captive by the Assyrian and Babylonian nations because of their idolatry. God compared this to adultery and a divorce (Jer 8:3; Is 54:7). For Paul, and the mission team, idolatry was not just an intellectual issue, it was a spiritual issue. It was not just an individual issue, it involved communities.

Paul mentioned that knowledge puffed up (made one conceited) but love/*agape* built up (encouraged others). Paul pushed the church to love others and be patient with "the vulnerable." He also mentioned that love was spiritual maturity, the better way, the mature way, and the best way for a community (1 Cor 13). Paul suggested that acting out of knowledge was not the best way (8:1). Christians were to act out of love. Love encourages others. Love also was the way to be known by God. Paul will later address spiritual issues (1 Cor 12 and 14) by indicating that *agape* causes the church to act for others. *Agape* causes Christians to act out of compassion, mercy, and empathy. Those Christians invited to eat meat offered to idols needed to act out of love and concern for others.

In 1 Cor 10:11 Paul suggested that these Christians had "arrived in the realm of maturity." Some have translated this phrase, "the fulfillment/end of the age has come." However, Paul indicated that these Christians were no longer part of the realm/age/empire that was passing away. They were members of the permanent/mature realm/age/empire of *agape* which is eternal. For Paul, the strong Christians needed to act out of love because they were in a realm of maturity and *agape*, not the realm of power, control, and oppression of the weak. They were not only acting out of "knowledge," they were guilty of oppressing the weak and therefore sinning against Jesus and their spiritual family.

Monotheism and the Web of Power

While we live in a time far away from Corinth it is important to understand why people struggled with polytheism. I have heard stories from missionaries concerning the difficulties in helping those raised in a polytheistic culture who believed in demon, deity, and idol worship. Letting go and believing in one God is difficult. Families pressure those who leave to remain faithful to their family traditions. People who step out of line are subject to persecution, family shunning, curses from the witchdoctor/priest/shaman, and the crises of faith that suggest they are sick because they left the truth. Monotheism is more than a choice; it is a reorienting of one's life. For many it is a difficult journey.

First, *since the ancient world believed in "spiritual balance" it was important to know the names of the gods, keep them happy, and use their power to confront those deities using evil on others*. Polytheism involved knowledge, power, manipulation, and submission. However, the call to follow one God helped ancient people *downsize* their lives and make them less complicated. A relationship with one God meant service and love to the one deity who controlled the world. It was simpler. However, in a complex culture built with an intricate web of polytheistic power, downsizing upset this web. This is why Paul called it a temporary empire. These were also the people who might persecute the Christians.

Second, *monotheism helped to bring focus to the lives of those in the ancient world*. Rather than seeking to learn and know many gods, the Almighty God helped one to place their focus on serving and growing closer to only God. Since this God was a god of love, the ancient follower did not have to worry about fear, manipulation, and power. God provided all of this and drew the believer closer in love. However, it separated the believer from a world dominated by power, fear, and manipulation.

The same issue was happening at Corinth. Paul mentioned that those who were struggling with polytheism had a "vulnerable/weak conscience" (8:7, 10, 11; 10:27). Those who seemed to minimize the dangers of polytheism acted out of knowledge (8:1, 7, 10, 11) rather than love. Paul suggested that they were acting for themselves (knowledge which puffs up) rather than for the benefit of others (love). Because of this those in the church who were weak were struggling, losing faith, or were falling into temptation. Paul's frustration was expressed by his statement that he would remove meat from his diet if it ever hurt others.

> "If food offends my brother (sister) then I won't eat in this realm so that I don't offend them." (8:13)

You Gotta Fight, For Your Right, to Party?

In the ancient world few people had rights. While the Roman Empire claimed to bring justice and peace (*Pax Romana*), they further enslaved most of the people. Those who had rights were Roman citizens, the wealthy, noble, and people in power. This consisted of three to five percent of the population. When discussions of rights and justice were held, it usually applied to a small group of people. Therefore, the majority of the community, as well as the majority of the church, could not be concerned about rights. They depended on those in power to defend and give them justice. However, those in power felt the need to protect their rights. In the ancient world, people succeeded by seizing power, honor, and rights from other people. To "give up" rights was not only risky, it was seen as a weakness. To be vulnerable was to lose power, honor, and status.

Instead of teaching the "weak/vulnerable" that idols were nothing, Paul called the "strong" to make sacrifices. As a mentor for the church he presented his ministry as an example. First, *while he and others on the team had the right to accept financial compensation from the church, they gave up that right*. While some suggest that Paul never received support from a local church, the Corinthian congregation seems to be the only one from which he refused support while in Corinth. He did take support from other churches and even requested more support as needed (Phil. 4). However, at Corinth Paul chose to work at his craft and accept help from churches in other places.

Second, *Paul mentioned that he intentionally made sacrifices for others so that they could be "won" for the Gospel*. This does not mean that Paul smoked pot with the pot smokers and shot heroin with the intravenous drug users, it meant that he made whatever sacrifice necessary to win those who were vulnerable. Instead of arguing about his rights he submitted himself to those whose fears kept them from seeing the true Gospel of freedom. Twice he mentioned that they did not use their rights (9:12, 15) and twice he mentioned that they became a slave to people and to the contest in the spiritual arena (9:19, 27). For Paul this commitment to others involve discipline, love, and concern. It was not about rights but about bringing others to maturity. Paul's comparison to the Corinthian sports events (9:24–27) illustrated that he was challenging the "strong" to make concessions for those who were struggling with fear, uncertainty, and commitment to Jesus.

Paul used himself as a model/type of leader (1 Cor 9). As one who had rights, honor, and status (as a Roman citizen) Paul was willing (even eager) to sacrifice his rights. He wanted others to be built up, saved, or accommodated. For Paul, his freedom was less important than other's salvation. He even described this sacrifice as a "discipline" much like the athletes (runners, boxers, and others) who denied themselves to win a crown of celery leaves (which withered after a few hours).

Submission for Others

1 Cor 9:1–6

> Am I not free?
> Am I not an apostle?
> Have I not seen Jesus our Lord?
> Are not you my workmanship in the Lord?
>
> If to others I am not an apostle, at least I am to you, for you are the seal of my apostleship in the Lord. This is my defense to those who would examine me.
>> Do we not have the right to eat and drink?
>> Do we not have the right to take along a believing wife,
>>> as do the other apostles and the brothers of the Lord and Cephas?
>>> Or is it only Barnabas and I who have no right to refrain from working for a living?

Paul seems to repeat phrases that may have been "catchphrases" among the Corinthian Christians as well as the culture. Some of these phrases may have been, "Am I not free?" "Everything is permissible," and phrases that involved "knowledge," and "freedom/rights." For the ministry team, Christianity was not about exercising one's rights or freedoms. Christianity was about helping, empowering, and building up others. One struggle may have been between the Jews and Gentiles in this church over dietary restrictions.

However, since Jesus freed people from food restrictions the Gentiles, who exercised little concern about food, would have felt comfortable in any setting. While some Gentiles would have struggled with rejecting polytheism and accepting the one true God, most saw this transition as a welcome lifestyle. Trying to keep the many gods, demons, and spiritual forces in balance created a sense of fear, paranoia, and despair. However, submitting to one god, who ruled the universe, would have become a type of "spiritual downsizing." Conversion to the Gospel of Jesus provided freedom from the many traditions and restrictions found in the religious community at Corinth. It also provided a sense of knowledge and power to the individual. To accept one God who ruled all creation and to serve that God through faith gave the believer a sense of power, hope, and freedom.

The nation of Israel was taken captive to Babylon in 586 BCE. The Babylonians surrounded Jerusalem, destroyed the walls, and desecrated the temple. The prophets claimed that this was the punishment of God and that God had appointed their king, Nebuchadnezzar as a servant to mete out justice. The Jewish nation was deported to Babylon for seventy years and lived as aliens in a foreign land. This happened because they had rebelled against God, worshipped idols, and forsaken the *Torah*. When the Jews returned home to rebuild their city and temple, they rededicated themselves to God's word, law, and covenant. As time developed and other nations tried to subjugate the nation of Israel, religious leaders placed tremendous emphasis on the Torah, the rejection of idolatry, and following eating regulations.

By the time of Jesus the Jewish nation had accepted the reality that the Roman's were ruling the world, however God had called them to protect the Torah, traditions, and worship of *Yahweh*. The Pharisees, Sadducees, lawyers, scribes, and elders of the people felt called to preserve the way of God in a world that was vastly different than they desired. Some groups such as the Dead Sea Scrolls community became monks and lived in the desert. They devoted their time to teaching, copying the sacred scrolls, and upholding rituals and purity rites for their community. Others lived in their communities and observed strict boundaries. Table fellowship was a touchy issue in this culture. Jesus was criticized over table, purification, and food regulations. Most Jewish people viewed dietary restrictions as a reflection of one's spirituality. It was very important that one exercised control in their eating. Even more, Gentiles were welcome in the Jewish home, but Jews needed to be cautious when invited to eat with a Gentile. The various food restrictions, religious rituals, and mixed relationships placed Jews and other cultures who valued dietary restrictions in a vulnerable position.

Concern about Temptation

1 Cor 9:19–27

> Even though I am free from all,
> > I have made myself a servant to all,
> > > that I might win more of them.
>
> > To the Jews I became as a Jew, in order to win Jews.
> > To those under the law I became as one under the law
> > > (even though I am not under the law) that I might win those under the law.

> To those outside the law I became as one outside the law
>> (not being outside the law of God but under the law of Christ) that I might win those outside the law.
> To the weak I became weak, that I might win the weak.
>
> I have become all things to all people, that by all means I might save some.
> I do it all for the sake of the gospel, that I may share with them in its blessings.
>
> Do you not know that in a race all the runners compete, but only one receives the prize? Run to get the prize. Every athlete exercises self-control in all things. They do it to receive a wreath that withers, but we one that lasts.
>
>> I do not run without a purpose;
>> I do not box as one punching the air.
>> I discipline my body and keep it under control, so that after preaching to others I am not disqualified

After explaining how involved idolatry has been in the history of the Jewish people, Paul attempted to create empathy in the reader concerning their past. The Jewish Christian's rejection of idols was not just historical, it was theological. To the Jew idols evoked an entire history of pain, suffering, and frustration for the Jewish nation. Rejection of idolatry was deeply ingrained in the Jewish individual. To be in the presence of an idol brought pressure from the Jew's community and their family. In this case guilt by association was a common problem for the Jewish Christian and Paul was sensitive to that. The Christian who felt that idols were nothing was also placing themselves and their church in a position of temptation.

Paul also asked them to use their knowledge to help others grow in Jesus. First, he mentioned that they needed to learn the history of the nation of Israel (For I do not want you to be ignorant . . .). Second, he reminded them that the stories of the punishment of Israel were examples for them to follow and absorb. Finally, they needed to "consider the people of Israel." For Paul the one who ate meat offered to idols was still playing with fire and needed to keep his eyes on those in the faith who were struggling. While it was a temptation to eat meat Paul reminded the Gentiles that others also would follow their actions.

> No temptation has taken you that is not human.
> God is faithful, and will not let you be tempted beyond your ability,
>> but with the temptation will provide the ability for a way out,
>>> so that you can endure.
>
> Therefore, my loved ones, run from idolatry.

Most people in the ancient world did not eat meat on a regular basis. Meat offered to idols was usually cooked to perfection and designed to be shared as a celebration. The palate was tempted by this occasional feast but Paul suggested that the Christian avoid this temptation. The temptation to engage in this social function also seemed important to the wealthy Christian. However, Paul suggested that they could avoid this temptation because God would care for them. God would always provide an option for them and would protect them from evil.

We many times forget how important food issues can be for others. In some countries food is scarce. People may hoard food as a means to provide for themselves and their families. In America, we have an abundance of food. For some Americans dietary restrictions dominate their lives. Those with health issues need to be cautious about their diets. Those who are survivors of trauma may be overcome with fear associated with body size, image, and may use food as a source of control. Others may use food as a source of comfort. Some have dietary restrictions due to spiritual convictions. Others choose certain foods due to a desire to live a healthier lifestyle. It is easy for some to see those with dietary restrictions as weak, unspiritual, and annoying. It is easy for those with dietary restrictions to see others as arrogant, lazy, weak, unspiritual, and unsympathetic.

Jesus came to set the captives free. In the gospels he intentionally violated many of the Jewish dietary restrictions and purity codes. For Jesus, all food was clean (Mark 7:19). He was responding to those who used food restrictions to judge others. Paul concurs in many other texts (Col 2:16; Rom 14:1–12) However, neither Paul (nor Jesus) ever intended food to become a spiritual battle (1 Cor 6:13). While spirituality and eating were many times equated with each other, it was never to be a test of fellowship or spirituality. For Paul:

- The mature Christian was to operate out of love rather than fear
- The mature Christian was to value relationship rather than rights

- The mature Christian was to use knowledge to understand others rather than judge them
- The mature Christian who loved others would be known by God

Follow my example

1 Cor 10:31 - 33

> Whether you eat
> whether you drink,
> Whether you do things,
> > do all to the glory of God.
> > > Don't become a problem to Jews, Greeks, and the God's community
>
> As I try to please everyone in what I do, not seeking my own benefit, but many so that they may be saved—be imitators of me, as I am of Christ.

At the end of this section Paul summarized the thoughts of the mission team. While those who were invited to dinner by the *Agonothete*, or others celebrating before their deity found this a temptation, Paul reminded them that they were expected to think of others. Whether it was a brother or sister who was vulnerable (struggling with idolatry), a dinner host who's conscience was devoted to that deity (10:28), or a Jewish Christian who honored the history of his nation by taking a strict stance against idols; Paul wanted the Corinthian Christians to operate out of love. This meant that they needed to think about the benefit of others rather than their own personal rights.

In this section, Paul seems to flesh out his major thought that is now expressed throughout the rest of the letter. *Agape* love is a sign of maturity, an opportunity to bless others, and a chance to be in harmony with God. Paul suggested that this love built up the community (8:1); sought the good of others (10:24); and put one in relationship with God (8:3). To love God is to be known by God and Paul suggested that spirituality in the faith community was less about knowledge than it was about loving and caring for others.

Every year we as a family attend Portland's Greek Festival. Our favorite experience at this festival involves standing in line amidst a large crowd of people by the "lamb table." The booth behind this table has six lamb carcasses rotating on a spit for six hours. The smell of charcoal, garlic, and roasted meat causes all our mouths to water. The anticipation of rich fatty meat brings a smile to everyone in line, including my boys. As the servers methodically disassemble the lamb carcass and announce the ticket number we move, as hypnotized carnivores, toward the table with our tickets. The smell of lamb now drives us forward as we watch the servers pile the meat onto small plates, smile, and take the ticket.

The rich lamb stimulates the happy chemicals to flood our brains and remind us that the money spent was well worth it. This past festival, which occurred as I was finalizing this manuscript, I had a horrid thought. What if the Apostle Paul came to us, placed his hand on our arms and, while smiling at the boys, said, "I know that this is good but are you aware that this lamb was sacrificed to Poseidon? I know you feel he is not a god, but see that family over there watching you? They thought they saw you bow when you took this meat. They think you were worshipping that god. Would you mind eating the spinach spanokopita or another batch of honey balls instead?"

How would I respond? "No way, I've waited a year for this and my happy chemicals are flowing. Besides—honey balls? Are you out of your mind?" I think 1 Cor 10:13 would apply here. We can resist and we can overcome. But even more, our compassion for others should drive us to sacrifice to help them grow closer to Jesus.

Supporting Others

This is not a text about drinking. It has been used to suggest that whenever we attempt to do something "controversial" we should err on the side of caution. However, this text has deeper meaning than that.

A few years ago I was in Albania on a mission trip. One of the young evangelists and I stopped for a drink. He ordered a Pepsi. I smiled because in the past many of the Albanians had a beer and offered me one. I was never one for drinking beer anyway because it doesn't appeal to me. I smiled at the young evangelist and said, "I'm buying so you get whatever you want." "I will take a Pepsi," he said. "OK, but if you want a beer that will be fine with me." He looked at me and said, "We have been told not to drink in front of the American missionaries." He looked very serious. I replied, "But I'm not weak in my faith so it doesn't bother me." He had a perplexed look on his face, almost as if the Albanians had always heard that they were the weak ones because they drank alcohol. I respected his commitment to hospitality so we had two cokes. We shared thoughts on this passage but I will always remember his response when I mentioned that the weak are those Christians who fear alcoholic beverages.

Paul provides a model for leadership in this section. While he had earlier modeled a willingness to do humiliating and menial tasks, here he modeled a willingness to sacrifice for others. In the Roman Empire rights were an important commodity. Yet Paul acknowledged a willingness to give up his rights for others. Again, the application is that if he was willing to do this, the Corinthian elite have no right to resist caring for the oppressed in the congregation. While it would require "passing up the meat plate and choosing the veggie platter" Paul suggests that this is the way of *agape*.

In light of Paul's sacrifice this is a small matter. As Paul had chosen not to be financially supported by the Corinthians. He and Barnabas (one of his companions in the earlier mission days) chose not to marry. While these were not wrong in themselves (actually Paul called them rights) Paul sacrificed them to help others. Too often churches forget that preachers have the right to be financially cared for and married. No church has the right to expect their leaders to be single or take a vow of poverty. This was strictly up to the individual.

The only model Paul was selling was one of sacrifice. While he was not asking others to be as extreme as he was, he was comparing his sacrifice to their small sacrifice of abstaining from meat for a meal. If Paul was willing to discipline himself to help others, they could do the same. In fact, it is interesting that he used the athletic games as his example of discipline. This image must have struck the Corinthian elite since their temptations occurred around the Isthmian games.

It is also important that Paul remind them that this sacrifice was to win others to Jesus. Christian leaders who act out of love and sacrifice present a great witness for Jesus. Paul was not suggesting that they "become like" those who were outside the empire of Jesus. He suggested that they serve and identify with those who did not know Jesus.

Understanding What It is To Be Weak/Vulnerable

Once I went to downtown Portland to minister to whomever God led to me. The public toilets, located at the heart of the city in Pioneer Courthouse Square were closed. This presented a problem for me because I typically use them since the businesses don't have public facilities. I drink a lot of coffee and try to meet people. Unfortunately this day I had only $1.50 in my pocket and needed to use the facilities. I asked some of the people on the street whom I knew where the next public restroom was. They laughed, "Ron, you're in Portland bro. You can use the street or the shelter." I found myself refusing to use the shelter. I held it until I found a place where I could buy coffee for under $1.50 and used their bathroom.

- I was embarrassed because I was ashamed to use the shelter bathroom
- I understood why people relieved themselves on the street, sidewalks, and alleys
- I almost wet myself because of my pride
- I wondered how many times this would have to happen for me to lose my pride
- I was angry because perfectly functioning bathrooms were unavailable to human beings
- I understood why they were locked and why business owners in the city are fed up with human waste on their sidewalks
- I came to appreciate the dilemma people face every day of their lives

I shared this in a sermon that Sunday. A man came to me afterward and said, "As someone who has been there and wet myself I appreciate that you told that story. It is humiliating. But no one seems to understand why."

Until we become like those we are trying to help we will never understand their pain, humiliation, and life. This is why the way of *agape* calls us to sacrifice. For a brief moment we have the opportunity to understand and in that understanding we realize—it's not about my rights. It's about their rights! It's a small sacrifice for me to make for their honor.

6

Empowering the Oppressed

OPPRESSED WOMEN

THE ROMAN GOVERNMENT PLACED a strong emphasis on order, especially concerning the practices of religious groups. Approved religious groups were monitored by the community leaders. Illegal religious groups may have met in secret and tried to avoid being discovered and shut down by the authorities. Stories were circulated concerning improper behavior by and toward males and females that caused local authorities to become anxious over these movements. Some of the concerns or stories involved:

- Females taking traditional male roles as priests, offering sacrifices, and killing the animal victims
- Gang rapes initiated by females who were in a "frenzy"
- Religious groups led by females, mostly slaves or prostitutes
- Females becoming violent towards males
- Males disturbing the accepted "order" in the community
- Mixing males and females except prostitutes and *heterai*

Proper Behavior

Corinth was emerging both as a Greek city and a spiritual center. The church was also emerging and enjoying freedom to assemble without persecution or harassment from the authorities. In Paul's letter to the Thessalonians he expressed concern that the Christians were facing social pressure from their community. This is not the case at Corinth where the Christian community seemed too comfortable with their outside community. Paul still, however, seems to suggest that the church must continue to avoid suspicion by outsiders.

Proper behavior was important in society concerning dress, public behavior, household codes, and moral behavior.[1] The pamphlet concerned dress, public behavior, household codes, and moral behavior. This had a tremendous effect on how religious groups were judged by Roman officials. Any group considered illegal (*religio illicita*) was closely watched by the authorities. Religious groups were concerned with correct performance and cult practice rather than morality and faith.[2] Keeping order in Roman colonies was an important task for city officials. In addition to various legal codes enforcing proper behavior was left to other community groups. *It was important for honorable individuals to follow proper social etiquette.*

Another method of enforcing appropriate behavior was the *gynaikonomoi*.[3] This group existed in Greece and consisted of *women who helped to monitor the behavior and dress of upper-class women*. The group at early Corinth monitored the temple cult of Aphrodite. The cult of Demeter also employed these women in the areas surrounding Corinth, even though the cult may have lost its influence in Paul's day. These women/messengers mainly made sure that respectable women acted appropriately. One area in which they focused was dress. Prostitutes tended to wear light, transparent garments. *Heterai* typically wore brightly colored clothing. Roman wives were expected to dress in the normal toga's that reflected their status in the community. They were expected to dress modestly, unlike other women who rebelled against "Roman family values." When the apostles Paul and Peter encouraged women to dress modestly (1 Tim 2:9; 1 Peter 3:1–6) they were encouraging the Christian women to exceed the current societal norms of their day.

After Caesar Augustus enacted his family reforms, see chapter four, his daughter Julia decided to rebel against her father's authority. She encouraged women to dress as *heterai* and prostitutes. She had sexual relations outside her marriage. She seemed to create a "new Roman woman" which suggested a rebellion to her father's reforms.[4] However, this new Roman

---

1. Winter, *After Paul Left*, 129.
2. de Vos, 52.
3. Winter, *Roman Wives*, 80–88.
4. Ibid., 43–51.

woman made Roman officials anxious. Keeping women modest was not only a concern for the Roman Empire, but the community as well.

Look Out for the Fashion Police

The *gynaikonomoi* or "fashion police," as I like to call them, had an important role. They made sure that respectable women acted and dressed respectably. Whether or not they were informants to the authorities is not known but they were the paparazzi of their day. In 1 Cor 11:10 Paul encouraged women to wear a head covering because of the angels or messengers (the Greek word has both meanings). It is possible that these messengers were the *gynaikonomoi* or other community representatives. In 1 Cor 14:23–25 he suggested that ungifted or non-members would enter the assembly. Because the church met in a home on Sunday, a day of business, people passing by the home could easily enter and stumble upon a worship service. They could also listen outside the window or the doorway. Paul seemed concerned about how the churches, especially women, were viewed by their community.

The cult of Dionysius was also affected by concerns for chaotic behavior. This concern led this religious group to forbid "tongue speaking," drunkenness, and disorderly conduct (sometimes displayed as frenzied or erratic behavior). Religious groups desired to maintain order, restrict women's behavior, and encourage socially accepted public behavior.[5]

Due to the anxiety that the Roman Empire displayed toward public behavior, Paul seemed protective of the church's reputation. While some might suggest that Paul was oppressive to women it seems more likely that he was protective of women and the church. If the Corinthian church's females were viewed as prostitutes, inappropriate, or suspected of immoral behavior the church and the women would become subject to legal and social pressures. If the church was viewed as disorderly or disrespectful, it might trigger persecution.[6] This letter suggests that the church did not experience conflict with outsiders. It seems likely that Paul would like this to continue.

---

5. Smith, 205.

6. de Vos suggests that persecution against the church was due to a local trigger event rather than an empire wide edict, 28.

1 Cor 11:2–16

I praise you because you remember me in everything and maintain the traditions as I passed them down to you.
But I want you to understand that
> the head of every man is Christ,
> the head of a wife is her husband,
> and the head of Christ is God.

Every man who prays or prophesies with his head covered shames his head

but every wife who prays or prophesies with her head uncovered shames her head
> it is the same as if her head were shaven.

If a woman will not cover her head, then she should cut her hair short.
> But since it is disgraceful for a wife to cut off her hair or shave her head,
>> she should cover her head.

A man should not to cover his head,
> since he is the image and glory of God,
> but woman is the glory of man.
> Man was not made from woman,
> but woman from man.
> Neither was man created for woman,
> but woman for man.
>> That is why a woman ought to have a symbol of authority on her head, because of the messengers.

In the Lord woman is not independent of man nor man of woman;
> as woman was made from man,
> so man is now born of woman.
> All things are from God.

Judge for yourselves: is it proper for a woman to pray to God with her head uncovered? Does not nature teach you that if a man wears long hair it is dishonorable for him, but if a woman has long hair, it is her glory? For her hair is given to her for a covering.

If anyone hassles us about this, we do not have a custom for this, nor do the churches of God.

Hoods and Togas

This passage of scripture has been controversial over the years. However, newer research has helped us to understand the issue Paul addressed at Corinth. For many years scholars suggested that Paul:

1. Was telling women to cover themselves with veils
2. Was suggesting that this displayed proper respect for their husbands

However, the many Roman coins, statues/busts, and writings that discuss "hoods" on the togas suggest that Roman males and females offered sacrifices and worshipped wearing a hood. The toga had a hood which those with status used during religious acts of religious devotion.[7] Many paintings depict both males and females wearing the hood during sacrifices. Augustus and Julius Caesar were also depicted on coins and statues wearing a hood. The hood suggested that Caesar was not only Lord, but a priest. When American television displays our president going to church, praying, or reading the Bible the same message is portrayed.

The hood seemed to be a sign of religious devotion. It was an act that both males and females practiced. In the church it seems that there once again was an issue with what was proper. First, *Paul seemed concerned with how women were viewed by society*. To wear the hood suggested devotion and to not wear it suggested disrespect. Winter indicates that women who did not cover their heads were viewed as prostitutes.[8] For men the issue was more divided. Jewish males were opposed to covering their heads while Romans were expecting to wear their hood in worship. One can imagine Sosthenes, Silas, Timothy, Paul, and Chloe's slaves discussing this issue and hotly debating both sides of the argument.

However, the issue also involved economic discrimination. Some authors suggest that hoods were a sign of status in the community; however this is a debated topic.[9] I would like to suggest that those who covered

---

7. Oster, "When Men Wore Veils," 500–501; *1 Corinthians*, 250; Witherington, 230–40.

8. Winter, *After Paul Left Corinth*, 120.

9. Rick Oster has given tremendous insight on the importance of hoods in Roman devotion and suggests that the hood displayed humility before the gods (*1 Corinthians*, 250), however other authors suggest that the hood was a sign of status (Clarke, *Secular and Christian*, 184, Jeffers, 42, Winter, 120).

their heads had status in Roman society. The team had the following issues to address:

- Wearing a hood was an expected sign of devotion and status for Roman citizens
- Women who should wear the hood but do not would be disgracing their partner and community
- Jewish men would not cover their heads and saw other males who did cover their heads as disrespectful
- Women needed to model modesty and respect in worship
- Women who spoke in the assembly would be suspect in the culture of others
- The poor were continually shamed in Corinth and needed to feel comfortable in the assembly
- Roman officials were also encouraged to serve as priests, which involved wearing a hood during religious services
- If women spoke in the assembly with a hood this would be acceptable
- If all men did not wear a hood in worship they would be equal
- If all women wore a hood they would be equal as well

Paul's solution seems complex. However, he and the team seem to suggest a uniform solution. All women should wear a hood when prophesying or praying. This would keep them respected in the eyes of the legal authorities and possibly the *glynaikonomoi*. It would also create an environment where all people felt empowered to worship without distinction. The men were not to wear a hood. Paul gave them a theological foundation, "They were in the image of God and should not hide their head." It also provided an opportunity for the upper-class males to model humility among the others in church. This humility was modeled by Jesus, expressed by the crucifixion (1:18–30).

Paul suggested that it was shameful for men to have long hair. For Paul, when men wore a hood (or had long hair) it was shameful conduct both culturally and theologically. Paul encouraged the women to respect the culture and submit. However, Paul encouraged the men to be somewhat counter-cultural.

This text does not "put women in their place." The text actually challenges men to practice humility in their spiritual community.

- In Roman culture males displayed power over other males.[10] In the empire of Jesus men with status should display humility and equality before God and other males.
- Women, like men, are to be in submission to authority
- Men reflect God's glory
- Men are to be the ones to challenge cultural norms
- Men reflect God's glory and humility by uncovering their head
- However, they would not make an issue of this, if anyone was contentious, the church was not making this a law
- The church needs to protect females and honor them in their communities
- Men were called to make the sacrifice and humble themselves among the poor

Hierarchy or Couplets

Sometimes we interpret 1 Cor 11 as suggesting that women are at the bottom of a pyramid. Paul's comments about head are typically diagrammed this way:

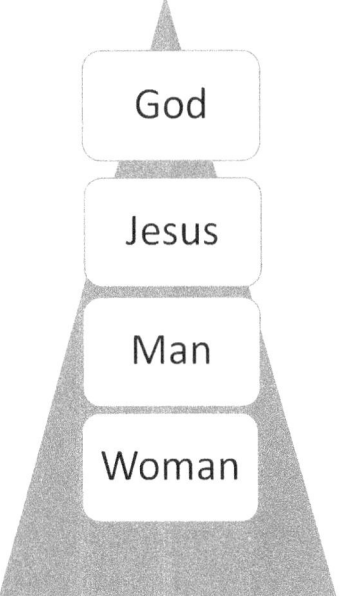

Figure 2: Hierarchy of Headship

---

10. Scott Bartchy, "Who Should Be Called Father," 31.

However, Paul speaks in couplets:

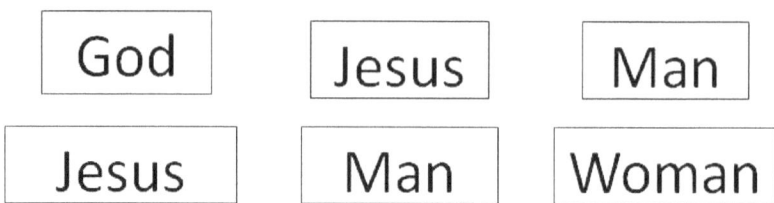

Figure 3: Couplets and Headship

This does not suggest that women are the bottom of the social scale, in the church. Headship is more than just authority or power. Headship carries responsibility. God is the head of Jesus. This suggests that God provides, cares for, and guides Jesus in their relationship. Likewise Jesus guides, nurtures, and leads males. However, because of the crucifixion (1 Cor 1:18–26) the head became vulnerable and humble. Men must also, as leaders, guide, nurture, develop, and manifest compassion for women and other men. Paul does not "put women in their place," Paul calls men to humility and to fulfill their responsibility. Paul also suggested that the "head" was honored through humility and sacrifices for others in the Christian assembly. Men, however, practiced headship by protecting women and modeling humility. Women honored the head by also practicing humility and submission.

This section of scripture was not written to address rebellious women and challenge them to be submissive. This section challenged both men and women to keep harmony in the church. These men and women needed to humble themselves in worship by removing promoting uniformity in the assembly with their hoods and embracing the poor in the church. In doing this they reflected their Lord Jesus, who humiliated himself on the cross for the oppressed at Corinth (1 Cor 1:18–23). For Paul and the mission team, the Corinthian Christians needed to keep peace in the congregation as a reflection of the unity and love of Jesus.

AGAPE, MEN, AND WOMEN IN THE CHURCH

Misogyny is a word that means a dislike or hatred of females. Too often churches operate out of misogyny rather than love and respect for females. Women are to be empowered to do ministry. Women have been confined to a seat on Sunday mornings, expected to be silent in any assembly, and have had to sit and watch baptized teenage boys lead prayers or pass communion. The church many times communicates to women that they are second class Christians. This section of scripture was not telling women to wear veils, hats, or keep their hair long. The text was first telling men to humble themselves by identifying with the poor, as Jesus had done. The church of *Agape* calls men to lead with humility.

Paul challenges Christian men to let go of their desire for status, power, and elitism in the community and seek humility before God and harmony with other men. In a culture of power Jesus calls Christian men to model unity and support for other males in the church. Women also are encouraged to live in harmony with their community by modeling humility, submission, and harmony in the church.

The Oppressed Poor

1 Cor 11:17–34

> In these instructions I cannot praise you because when you gather it is not for the better but for the worse. First, when you gather as an assembly I hear that there are divisions among you and I partly believe it.
>
> It is necessary for there to be groups among you so that those who are approved can be shown.
>
> When you gather it is not the Lord's dinner you eat. For each takes their own dinner and eats it, some are full and others drunk.
>
> Can't you eat and drink at home or is God's assembly dishonorable where you can humiliate those who have nothing.
>
> Should I praise you for this?
> I won't!
>
> I received from the Lord what I gave to you. The night that Jesus was betrayed/delivered over he:
>   took bread,
>   gave thanks,
>   broke it,
>   and said, "This is my body for you, eat this to remember me."
> In a similar manner he:

> took the cup, after supper,
> and said, "This cup is the new covenant in my blood, do this when you drink it to remember me."

> When you eat this bread and drink the cup you proclaim the Lord's death until he comes. Whoever eats this bread and drinks the cup in an unworthy way is guilty of despising the Lord's body and blood.

> Each one should test themselves concerning how they eat and drink [in this assembly]. The one who does not compare themselves in the body eats and drinks condemnation on themselves, this is why
> > some are hungry,
> > some are sick,
> > some fall asleep.

> If we make distinctions we will not be judged. When we are judged by the Lord we are disciplined so that we may not be condemned along with the world.

> When you gather to eat, wait for each other.
> > If someone is hungry—eat at home.
> > That way you will not be condemned when you gather.

> I will explain the rest when I come.

This situation at Corinth was affecting those who were doing "without." Paul was concerned with their observation of the "Lord's dinner." This can suggest two problems in the Corinthian congregation. First, *it may refer to the celebration of Jesus' last meal with his disciples.* The Lord's dinner refers to Jesus' last supper found in the Gospels. Jesus shared a Passover meal with his disciples and then participated in the Thanksgiving meal (*Todah*) after this Passover. The Thanksgiving meal was usually after the Passover and consisted of bread and wine. In the Gospels there is no mention of meat. There is only bread and wine. Luke 22:20, mentions that Jesus lifted the cup a "second time," which was a symbol at Roman meals, that a new stage in the dinner had begun.

Second, *Paul may be referring to a meal which the Corinthian Christians celebrated together during the day of their worship.* Usually gatherings would include a meal in the host's home. Meals were viewed as a spiritual time in which a god was invoked, blessed, and honored. When the cup of wine was passed Zeus, Dionysius, or another god was thought to be present during meal suggesting that this was a divine activity. It is possible that these Christians called it the Lord's dinner because they expected Jesus to be present. This could have been before or during their Sunday worship, since that was the most convenient time to assemble. Whichever reason Paul wrote, his point was that people were being neglected and mistreated. This, Paul believed, was taking the Lord's meal inappropriately. It was profaning Jesus' body (the church) and blood. Paul also believed that the church should wait for each other.

Roman Meals

Probably the one element in the Greek and Roman cultures that stayed consistent throughout the centuries was the meal or banquet (called the symposium). In Paul's time the Roman meal consisted of different stages. Roman elites usually slept late, went to the baths or the gymnasium, and received an invite to a home for dinner.[11] During the heat of the day they came to a dinner which lasted many hours.

The first stage was the meal. The Roman meal began with wine and appetizers. Then the dinner guests ate together for the main course. After this they began the second cups, or the Symposium. During this time dinner guests drank, discussed philosophy, danced, and many times continued into late hours of the night. Singing to the gods was also an important part of the meal. Usually Zeus or Dionysius was the god of choice for worship. Musonius Rufus mentions that during this time many sins were committed.[12] In Plato's tract, *Symposium*, Socrates stated that the group had spent the previous night in drunkenness. This night, the night of the *Symposium*, they were going to focus on philosophy. Other symposiums involved prostitution with male and female slaves, sexual orgies, and fights.

Traditionally women were excluded from the dinner, unless they were prostitutes, slaves, or *heterai*.[13]

> The presence of an unveiled woman accompanied by a man in public signaled that she might not be his wife. At a typical banquet a woman (not necessarily his wife) seated next to a married man would be his social and sexual companion, *hetaira*, for that evening.[14]

---

11. Osiek and Balch, 200.
12. Oster, *1 Corinthians*, 265.
13. Osiek and Balch, 45.
14. Winter, *After Paul*, 127–28.

> If women were present, they would be either flute girls or *hetairai* . . . That is to say, they would have a subservient role, primarily one in which they were treated as sexual objects. Indeed, one of the institutional features of the symposium tradition was the motif of violence against women.[15]

Those who were poor or slaves were sent to another dining room much more crowded, dark, and served substandard food. Patrons invited their clients to dinner many times just to humiliate them. The meal was a very traditional element that consistently upheld proper etiquette. Guests were invited early in the day and came from afternoon until late evening.

When Jesus offered the second cup during his last dinner he signaled that the early Christians could treat the meal as a symposium. However, this was a time of fellowship, worship, and teaching rather than time for immorality and drunkenness.

Peter Lampe has done excellent research on both the Roman meal and potlucks.[16] Potlucks were a common practice in the ancient world because people were allowed to bring their own food to share with others during the meal.[17] The Roman potluck was supposed to be a time of sharing and communion where all those in attendance were able to eat, drink, and be happy. Even the poor, who were lucky enough to be invited, were fed by those who brought more food than normal. Socrates was concerned about the abuses of this meal since many people brought their own food but would not share with the poor who were in attendance. This was an abuse of the fellowship meal. In some cases the wealthy (who did not work during the day) came early and ate their fill. When the poor arrived later, without food, they went hungry. The early church father John Chrysostom suggested that in this text the Corinthians did not share with the needy and ate by themselves.[18]

An Invitation to Dinner

Not only were the poor neglected, they were many times humiliated. The Roman satirist Juvenal tells the story of being invited to a patron's home for a dinner. He states that, "You would be better off eating scraps . . ." Juvenal's account depicts the poor client who is confined to a small room

---

15. Smith, 42.
16. Peter Lampe, "The Corinthian Eucharistic Dinner Party," 1–16.
17. Ibid., 10.
18. John Chrysostom, *Proem NPNF* 1: 12:1–2.

to eat hard bread, nasty fish, and drink old wine.[19] However, he observed that the host and his favored guests ate the finest food while the clients ate substandard food, were injured in a brawl, and were mistreated by slaves. In addition to Juvenal's account, honored guests were arranged such that they sat together in the best seats and best company. This also was another method of humiliating those who were without.[20]

The classical texts teach us something about proper behavior at Roman meals. First, they were very traditional and exclusive of proper women, the poor, and slaves. Second, they had a habit of becoming a place for sin, drunkenness, immorality, fights, and mistreatment of the poor. Finally, those who worked throughout the day usually arrived after the meal and had to only eat bread and wine until the late hours of the night. This humiliated those without status, food, or money.

The Symposium, while a wonderful time of fellowship for the wealthy, became a time of sacrifice and humiliation for those without. The poor either watched others eat or were sent to a dark room in the home to eat the nasty food unfit for the special guests.

What was happening at Corinth?

Paul was not happy with what was happening during the meal (11:21, 33). First, Paul accused them of humiliating the poor (11:22). Second, he suggested that some were weak, not enough food, and others were falling asleep, too much food and wine (11:21, 33).[21] The worship service was no longer a time of sharing, fellowship, and worship. It was a time when those with status were neglecting and humiliating those without.

Paul believed that this problem supported his underlying accusation that they were discriminating against and neglecting the poor in the congregation. Paul suggested that the Christians wait for each other (11:33). The word for wait/receive is used in the Greek Old Testament for hospitality.[22] While the wealthy would have been invited to dine in the early afternoon, the poor would have been working until the early evening. Since the upper class felt it was beneath them to work, they were able to sleep until late in the morning, visit the bathhouses, discuss knowledge at the

---

19. Juvenal, *Satires*, V.
20. Osiek and Balch, 195; Smith, 33.
21. Smith, 201.
22. Winter, *After Paul Left Corinth*, 151.

town square, and then arrive for dinner in the early afternoon. However, the poor did not have this leisure.

Paul suggested that the wealthy wait to eat until the others arrived. He wanted the Lord's Supper to be a time to care for the body of Christ and feed the poor. The common practice in society of neglecting the poor was happening in the church. While many have focused on "examining oneself" (11:8) and partaking without recognizing the body of the Lord (11:28-29) as personal reflection the context also suggests that this can apply to the larger body. Each Christian needed to examine themselves in the body (church/congregation), which reflected how they treated their poor brothers and sisters. For Paul this time was a time when all people were to be equal. He is expanding on his theme in chapters eight through ten concerning sacrificing for the weak. He also extended this theme to the assembly concerning hoods (distinctions between classes and sexes, 11:1-16); feeding the poor (11:17-34); and spirituality (12-14).

The Lord's Supper Today

Too often we treat the Lord's Supper as our own personal time with God. We take our individual cracker and our individual juice glass and spend time with our thoughts. Others go to a table and dip their own piece of bread in a glass of wine and eat it by themselves. Some go to the front of a church and have the priest/pastor place an individual wafer on their tongue and let them sip from a large goblet of wine. In these instances communion becomes an individual act. One man once told me how he was frustrated because the people around him were making noise (children, parents) and that they were interrupting his communion with his God!

When Paul stated that people should examine themselves it can mean personal reflection. If I sin, I can't take communion. If I feel unworthy, I better pass. If I haven't confessed my faults, I better do it before the bread plate comes to me or I will have to wait until next week (or Sunday night if I am lucky). However, we are also to examine ourselves by recognizing the body. This means that we acknowledge or accept those in Jesus, especially the poor and oppressed among us.

Yet communion has never been only an individual process. The word communion means "fellowship." It also involves being an active part of a group. In this chapter Paul suggests that examining ourselves means we observe our relationship in the body of Christ. Paul actually warns us about individual worship (1 Cor 14:28). Worship exists within the body of Christ. The man, mentioned earlier, who was concerned about children making noise, during his private communion time, may have been a better example if he could have turned to the woman next to him, who was wrestling her three children, served her communion, and helped the kids feel comfortable.

Paul, in this text, suggests that communion is about our relationship with God and others. Paul focused on the dynamics of the body. At Agape we have tried to keep our communion service simple and a copy of our early beginnings in a home. First, in Acts 20:7 the early church communed every Sunday. Second, since communion was part of a meal, we wanted to keep the same feel we had in a home. Since Jesus asked that all be invited to the table (Luke 14:12–24) we invite all to join us in communion. Finally, since conversation was part of the early symposium, we try to make our communion more dialogue and celebration.

Many times our people share stories about their relapse or temptation to relapse into their addictions of choice. We share successes, failures, and struggles. We are a community and communion invites all people to not only join in the meal but the discussion and the fellowship as well. I have also been amazed at how many others listen to the conversations and are challenged in their own faith, hypocrisy, spiritual growth, struggles, and view of God. Communion is not only about my relationship with God but also our relationship with each other. It calls for empathy rather than focus. It means that we prepare our minds and hearts by listening to others rather than shutting the world out.

Our commitment to communion extends past local poverty. Christians who commune each Sunday should not forget that this is a global phenomenon. Just as we are called to wait for those locally, we must make sure that those globally receive their nourishment and food. While we cannot end world poverty it is important that we see communion as a worldwide worship and be concerned about those who join us at the table of fellowship. It also provides an opportunity for us to talk about our Christian family in other countries struggling with poverty, globalism, and oppression. In this way we not only examine ourselves in the local body but the global body as well.

7

Spiritual Power

A STORY ABOUT THE BODY

THE HISTORIAN LIVY, WROTE about a Roman leader, Menenius Agrippa (494 BCE), who obtained honor by encouraging his soldiers to stay with the army during a battle. In the story the citizens would not cooperate with the leaders (patrons) by supporting the army and going to war. Menenius shared with them a parable of the body, how the members did not acknowledge the stomach which stopped working, and how the body suffered because the stomach refused to work. The parable was a reminder that the body needed to work as a team in order to survive.[1]

In the Greek world democracy was common practice. Leaders were chosen, by the people, and for the people. The leaders' power rested in their ability to persuade and inform the community (this form of leadership is similar in the church) to make good choices. The community was *called* into an assembly where the leaders spoke to the group. Their skills in speech, personal ethics, and passion for the issue were important in informing the community. The gods oversaw the city and directed the affairs of the people through these leaders.[2] This was democracy.

When Rome seized the Greek cities democracy ceased. Leaders were chosen by Rome and informed the assembly of Caesar's edicts, laws, and statutes. The people had little voice in this government. Democracy was viewed as messy business. The people could not be allowed to be involved in divine business of the government. People were encouraged to submit

---

1. Livy, *Ab Urbe Condita Libri*: 2. 16, 32, 33.; Xenophon, *Memor.* 2.3.18, and Cicero, *Duties* 3.5.22.

2. Clarke, *First Century Christians*, 21.

and accept the laws of Rome. Agrippa's story suggested that the body parts (people) support, submit, and yield to the will of the head or leadership. His writing also suggested that unity in the community was something leadership must cultivate.

1 Cor 12:1–11

> Brothers and sisters, I don't want you to be uninformed concerning spirituality.
>
> We know that when you were gentiles you were led by idols that could not speak. You should know that no one speaking by God's spirit says that Jesus is cursed.
>
> No one can say that Jesus is lord except by the Holy Spirit.
>
> There are diverse gifts but one spirit.
> There are diverse ministries but one lord.
> There are diverse powers but one God,
> > the one working in everything everywhere.
>
> The spirit is displayed in each one for the common good.
> > To one the spirit gives a word of wisdom,
> > to another a word of knowledge according to the same spirit.
> > To others faith by the same spirit,
> > to another gifts of healing by the one spirit,
> > to another works of power,
> > to another a prophecy,
> > to another the ability to distinguish spirituality,
> > to another different languages,
> > to another the ability to interpret languages.
>
> All of these are the work of one spirit who gives to each as it wishes.

A STORY ABOUT SPIRITUALITY

In this section Paul addressed another important issue in the Corinthian church. The issue was not spiritual gifts, as some commentators suggest. Actually the world *gift* does not occur in the text. The word is simply "spirituality," or "spiritual things/issues." The church was obviously struggling over those who felt more spiritual in the body. Based on the social evidence at Corinth we can safely assume that some were claiming superiority over others.

The word spirituality is a reoccurring theme in this letter.

- 2:14–15 Spiritual ones have the mind of Christ (humility) rather than that of the world
- 3:1 Spirituality is maturity

Paul has consistently suggested that spirituality was expressed by caring for others and loving or giving to the oppressed. In our text Paul addressed *spirituality* rather than *spiritual gifts*.

First, *Paul acknowledged that most of the Corinthians' experience of the divine was rooted in idolatry, ecstatic speech, and curses.* In the ancient religions of Paul's day these were three common themes. Idols represented the image and presence of a god. Some gods and goddesses came in the form of humans, animals, planets/stars, or other bodies. Statues were built to capture these representations or depict scenes from stories of the gods. By worshipping the statue or at the temple people thought that they were experiencing these divinities and their spiritual manifestation.

Those who spoke for the gods were priests, oracles, prophets, or seers. Ecstatic speech was one medium of this communication. Since the high majority of the populations were illiterate, the messages and stories of these gods were delivered orally. Speech that was repetitious, unrecognizable or a command from the god was the main medium of communication. Those who could speak for a god were viewed as divine messengers. Ecstatic utterance, frenzied behavior, and overwhelming emotion gave the illusion of power to others. These qualities suggested that the person became inhabited by the god and was a vessel for this diving being. Today's voodoo religions are not far removed from this religious behavior. However, most religious cults (including the cult of Dionysius) did not include ecstatic speech in their meetings.[3]

Curses were an important method of control among religious communities. The world of polytheism required that religious leaders know the names of gods, characteristics, and ways to control their sphere of influence. Medicines, incantations, and formula prayers gave the person power. Repetitious phrases were used to waken or rouse the divine beings. However, saying the name of a god gave the speaker a sense of control and power.

---

3. Smith, 205.

Second, *in the ancient world power, knowledge, and control reflected one's spirituality.* The mystery religions provided rich and poor an initiation into the knowledge of the story and life of the god. Knowledge gave them power, respect, honor, and awe. Even though religion was shifting at Corinth, the lower classes still believed and promoted their devotion to deities.

Paul suggested that the pagan form of spirituality was far removed from the true God. In chapter two Paul wrote that Jesus represented the wisdom of God. This wisdom was manifested by humility, sacrifice, suffering, and shame. Throughout 1 Corinthians Paul has also suggested that spiritual maturity was manifested through loving others, sacrifice, and self control. To love was the way to know and be known by God (1 Cor 8:1–3). Knowledge, relationship, and a spiritual connection with God came through relationship with others.

A painting has been uncovered on a household wall in the ancient city of Pompeii.[4] Pompeii was a Roman city buried by volcanic ash when Mt. Vesuvius erupted around 79 CE. The painting depicts a rite of passage for the mystery religion of Dionysius (god of wine). The initiate saw the story of Dionysius death acted out, experienced a sexual encounter, was physically beaten, and then (on the final scene) looked into a mirror at their face. While mirrors in the ancient world provided poor reflections, this religion suggested that the initiate was now transformed by the knowledge and participation in the story. While this is a painting it suggests some themes common in ancient religions.

A Story About Hierarchy and the Church

In 1 Corinthians 12 Paul's speech on the body was similar to Menenius Agrippa's fable. Paul mentioned that the weaker members should receive more honor and protection. As the body worked together to protect the weaker parts (crotch, chest, extremities) so the community of Jesus needed to work together to protect the vulnerable. Agrippa suggested that the leaders could not force the "plebes" to go against their will. Both Paul's and Agrippa's parables suggested that the strong work with the weak.

Paul mentioned that while the church had various gifts, they were designed to support the body and work together (12:4–11). In pagan religion power gifts were the most important manifestations of spirituality

---

4. Nappo, 154–57.

and divine power. However, in the church this was reversed. Paul suggested that the gifts that involved leadership and building up the body of Christ were most important. These gifts were missionaries, prophets/preachers, teachers, and those who encouraged others in the body. Paul sought to change how the Corinthian Christians saw other people in the church. As he had done earlier in the letter Paul tried to turn their view of reality upside down. Their typical view of spirituality (power gifts) was part of the *oikoumenē*, which was vanishing away (13:1, 2, 8). Their new world, the empire of God, viewed spirituality differently. Spirituality involved loving others and building up people. Spirituality was produced through *agape*.

Power Gifts	New Spirituality
Paganism	Christian empire
Elevation of the individual—languages/ecstatic speech	Mission of the church—prophecy and interpretation which encourages others
Led by mute idols	God and spirit place gifts to support the weak
Ignorance	Works with spirit of God and mind
Spirituality = power and self	Spirituality = *agape* and helping others

Figure 4: Comparison of Power Gifts and New Spirituality Paul suggested that the divine force in this new community was *agape* love.

Agape

1 Cor 12:27–13:1

> The body is not one member, but many.
> If the foot said:
> > "Because I am not a hand I am not a member of the body,"
> > > it would still be part of the body.
> If the ear said:
> > "Because I am not an eye I am not part of the body,"
> > > it would still be part of the body.
> If the whole body were an eye,
> > how would it hear?
> If it were an ear,

how would it smell?

The members in the body have been placed according to God's will. If they were all one part (all the same) what would happened to the body?
That is why there are many members and one body.
The eye can't say to the hand,
"I don't need you."
The head cannot say to the feet,
"I don't need you."
Those weaker members of the body are necessary. Those dishonorable [modest] parts of the body we treat with modesty but we do not worry about the presentable parts. God blended the body and has given greater honor to the weak so that it will not be divided but will care for each member.

If one suffers—all suffer.
If one is honored—all rejoice with it.

You are the body of Christ and members of it. God has placed in the church:
first apostles
second prophets
third teachers
    then powers
    then gifts of healing
    then helpers
    then administrators
    then languages

Everyone is not an apostle.
Everyone is not a prophet.
Everyone is not a teacher.
Everyone is not a power worker.
Everyone does not have gifts of healing.
Everyone does not speak in languages.
Everyone does not interpret.

Seek the greatest gift. I will display the better way for you.

In ancient Greek and Roman schools, advanced education involved composing various forms of literature. One form designed to elicit praise was the *encomium*. *Encomiums* were small biographies of individuals. These biographies consisted of a character, the history of the individual, why they should be praised, and their qualities that were noteworthy.

Many scholars suggest that the Gospels were ancient *encomiums* designed to praise the life of Jesus. The *encomium* was a basic composition much like our own historical character reports written in secondary school.

Encomiums were also written about virtues such as grace, mercy, love, peace, and others. These virtues were described as invaluable and worthy of praise. As a Pharisee, Paul would have been educated in the Greek language and literature. His scribe (for this letter) would also have been trained in writing the basic *encomium*. 1 Cor 13 seems to be similar to one of these *enconiums* devoted to virtues rather than individuals. One can imagine Paul and the team composing this together and sharing a common educational tool. This *encomium* would be the major thought of the letter. This virtue, *agape*, would also become a common thread throughout the text. In this context Paul's *encomium*/composition described the greatest gift. The greatest gift is *agape*/love.

1 Cor 13:1–13

> If I speak in languages of men and angels
> but don't have *agape*/love
> > I am a banging gong or loud cymbals
>
> If I have prophecy and knowledge of mysteries and all knowledge
> and have faith to move mountains
> > but don't have *agape*
> > > I am nothing
>
> If I give away all I own and give my body to boast
> > but don't have *agape*
> > > I gain nothing
>
> *Agape* is:
> > patient
> > kind
>
> *Agape* is not:
> > boastful
> > arrogant
> > shameful
> > provoked to anger easily
> > focused on the bad
> > > it rejoices in righteousness
> > > it bears everything
> > > it believes all
> > > it hopes in everything
> > > it endures all

> *agape* does not fail
>> prophecies will pass away
>> languages will cease
>> knowledge will pass away
>
> We have incomplete knowledge
> we have incomplete prophecies
> but when the maturity comes
>> incompleteness passes away
>
> When I was a child
>> I spoke like a child
>> I thought like a child
>> I reasoned like a child
>>> but when I grew up
>>>> childishness passed away
>> Because we look into a mirror, we see an enigma.
> Then we see face to face.
>> We have incomplete knowledge.
> Then we will know as we have been known.
>
> These three remain
>> faith
>> hope
>> *agape*
>>> *Agape* is the greatest of these three.

Paul explained, in 1 Cor 13, why *agape* is the greatest.

- Love makes life/faith complete
- It is a noble virtue
    - It is patient
    - It is kind
    - It is not arrogant or focused on self
    - It does not mistreat others
    - It endures
    - It does not end/is eternal
    - It is complete/mature

Paul mentioned that love/*agape* was the component of spirituality that produced permanence. Love made the gifts of knowledge (13:2; 8:1–3), prophesy (13:2, 14:1–26), and languages mature. Love was the virtue of spirituality that causes us to mature. In Matt 5:43–48 Jesus suggested that God is mature because God loves the good and the bad unconditionally.

Paul compared the physical growth process to spiritual maturity. Children act as children. Then they mature and act as adults. This maturing process Paul called "putting away childishness." The word for "putting away" is used often in 1 Corinthians and translated abolished or passing away.

- 1:28; 2:6 The world is passing away
- 2:8 Rulers are passing
- 7:31 The world in present form is passing away
- 13:11 Childhood passes away

The terms passing away and abolished are the same Greek word. They denote the temporary or the part of the world that is in transition. However, the empire of God is mature/complete/perfect. It is that part of the world which endures or lasts. *Agape* is the major characteristic of this kingdom because it also lasts, endures, and is complete.

Paul mentioned that wisdom, prophecy, knowledge, and languages were part of that "temporary" empire (13:8). They belong to that immature realm which needed *agape* in order to be effective. They were also lord of the temporary realm of religion, power, and control. Paul was not suggesting *when* they would cease, end, or be abolished. Paul only suggested *that* they were not part of the realm of love, maturity, and completeness.

Some suggest that languages/tongues refer to the ecstatic utterances found in many ancient religions. While this may be partly true, the word simply means *languages*. Corinth was a port city and multilingual. Whether the languages were considered real languages or ecstatic utterances (similar to those found in modern Pentecostalism, charismatic movements, voodoo cults, or charismatic segments of the Hindu faith) the point that Paul made suggests that this gift, which was considered a sign of intellectual superiority or power over others, was not part of the enduring realm.

What about tongues of angels (13:1)? In all literature, that I have read or researched, only the Jewish *fable The Testament of Job* (*Test Job* 48–50) refers to this practice. In the story Job's daughters speak in the "tongues of angels." This does not suggest any real phenomena, it was only a myth. Paul, however, began his thought in 1 Cor 13 with statements; "If I speak in the tongues/languages of men or angels . . . " "If I have the gift of prophecy . . . " "If I have faith that can move mountains . . . " or "If I give all I possess to the poor . . . " Paul does not suggest that languages of angels were real phenomena. He only suggested that whatever he did could only be complete or spiritually mature if it was done with love/*agape*.

There have also been questions concerning "that which is perfect." (13:10). Some indicate that this refers to Jesus. The thought is that when he "who is perfect" comes, these gifts will cease. Therefore since Jesus has not come, the gifts *must* continue to be practiced in the church. Others have suggested that this refers to the Bible/scriptures/law of Jesus. James 1:25 tells us "The one who looks intently into the perfect/mature law that gives freedom. . ." This view, and the accompanying verse, suggests that when the Bible was officially adopted as scripture, the scriptures were complete/perfect. Therefore the gifts would no longer be needed, since their purpose was to confirm the word/message of the church. A third suggestion is that "that which is perfect. . ." refers to the church's maturity. When the early church grew and became stable (mature) the spiritual gifts were no longer necessary.

I believe that none of these explanations completely explain what "that which is perfect" was meant to convey. First, Paul has not been concerned with "when" the temporary was abolished but "that" the temporary would be abolished. He suggested that the empire of God co-exists in this temporary world and that the Christians mature and live in these two realms. His discussion was spatial rather than chronological. Paul was not suggesting that the power gifts end, he suggested that they have power only in a fading world that gives them authority. However, faith, hope, and love flourish in the permanent/mature empire (13:13).

The term "perfect" also means mature or complete. Throughout Paul's writings he used this word for maturity (Eph 4:12–16; Phil 3:17; Col 3:14; 4:12). Not only did Paul believe that love was the fruit of maturity, it brought one into an intimate relationship with God. As mentioned earlier many mystery religions used crude mirrors (usually made out of Corinthian bronze) to symbolize the reflection and glory of an encounter with the god. For Paul *agape* brought one to see God face to face. This face to face meeting does not suggest the resurrection or afterlife. It refers to the relationship Moses had with God, and one that all Christians can have.

> Yahweh used to speak to Moses face to face, as a man speaks to his friend. When Moses turned to those in the camp, his assistant Joshua the son of Nun, a young man, would not depart from the tent. (Exod 33:11)

> I clearly speak mouth to mouth with him [Moses], not in an enigma, and he observes the form of Yahweh. Why were you not afraid to speak against my servant Moses?" (Num 12:8)

These texts suggest that Moses' relationship with God was both prophetic and intimate. God did not want Moses to see an enigma (similar to 1 Cor 13:12) but the glory and love of God in relationship. Paul also referred to this relationship in 2 Corinthians.

> When one turns to the Lord, the veil is removed. The Lord is the Spirit, and where the Spirit of the Lord is, freedom exists. All of us observe the glory of the Lord without a veil on our face and are being transformed into the same image from one degree of glory to another. This comes from the Lord who is the Spirit. (2 Cor 3:16–18)

Paul stressed to the Corinthians that practicing *agape* rather than knowledge and power gifts brought them into relationship with God and reflected true spirituality and spiritual maturity.

> If anyone thinks that they know something, they do not yet know as they should. If anyone loves God, they are known by God. (1 Cor 8:2–3)

In 1 Cor 13 Paul not only has composed an *encomium* to *agape*, he has stated that *agape* is mature, stable, and enduring. The context of 1 Corinthians does not concern the coming of Jesus or the institution of the scriptures. The chapter concerns *agape*. The chapter also does not tell us that *agape* causes the gifts to end. It tells us that *agape* is the greatest and stable gift and one that should be the motivation and maturing quality of the Corinthian Christians. It belongs in the permanent empire of Jesus.

Paul has been addressing problems in the congregation concerning selfishness, arrogance, and discrimination among the Christians. For Paul, some were elevating themselves spiritually over others. More than likely these "spiritual" ones were the wealthy, educated, and social elite. However, Paul has been suggesting that the "spiritual" ones operate out of love for others including the lower class. They were those who identify with the oppressed and humiliated, respected the opposite sex, had empathy for others who struggled with polytheism, and altered their public behavior for the poor. Here, they were to help and love others more than themselves.

Spiritual abuse is very common among faith communities. Spiritual abuse happens when oppressive and controlling people use religion as a vehicle to further oppress others. The problem at Corinth was that spirituality had become a way/tool to extend the abusers' power and control. However, spiritual abuse does not care about others but oneself. In 1 Cor 13 Paul suggested that *agape* prevents spiritual abuse. Spiritual abuse is selfish, arrogant, narcissistic, and controlling. Love is the opposite. Love cares for others and builds them up. There is no abuse in love because love seeks to better others.

Agape in Worship

In 1 Cor 14 Paul applied this concept of *agape* to the church assembly. We have already discussed how their assembly had reflected the sins of social segregation that existed in their community. Paul had reminded them (5:3; 11:18) that their assemblies were not a reflection of his way of life and teaching. Paul expressed disapproval over what was happening in the worship. However, he was concerned about their social relationships rather than their acts of worship. In this chapter he applied the practice of *agape* as a gift present in their worship and a sign of spirituality.

1 Cor 14:1–5

> Pursue love
> Seek spirituality
> even more, prophesy
>
> The one who speaks in a language does not speak to people but to God because no one hears them and they speak spiritual mysteries.
>
> The one who prophesies to people speaks to build them up, encourage, and support them.
>
> The one speaking in a language builds themselves up.
>
> I want all of you to speak in languages but I'd rather you prophesy because the one who prophesies is greater than the one who speaks in a language—unless someone interprets so that the church may be encouraged.

First, *Paul downplayed the use and practice of "speaking in languages" in the assembly.* Paul did suggest that they not forbid/prevent the practice of these tongues. However, Paul does not elevate this gift but seems to suggest that it be minimized in the assembly. While some may use 1 Cor 12–14 as support for tongues, Paul was not positive concerning its practice. He may be addressing both languages and ecstatic utterances but he is highly critical of any language that cannot be understood by others (14:9–11). Paul wrote that these languages build up the speaker (14:4), were not understandable to some of those attending the assembly (14:2), needed to be interpreted (14:13), caused the mind to be unfruitful (14:14), did not build up others (14:17), and were a sign for unbelievers—suggesting that they be used within the community (14:22). Paul also suggested that the speaker should keep quiet or speak to themselves and God, if there were no interpreter available (14:28). These comments do not reflect a positive attitude concerning "speaking in languages/tongues." Paul was very critical of this "gift" or manifestation of "spirituality" in the church. To encourage someone to speak to themselves and God suggested isolation from the community, which was not the way of *agape* (14:28).

Since these languages/tongues, as well as those using this gift had little use in the church, they did not reflect the true heart of *agape*. Love does not build up oneself; it seeks to build up others. Languages/tongues builds up the individual which is the opposite of *agape* (14:1–2). While Paul encouraged the church not to discourage those who spoke in languages/tongues, the church was expected to focus on others. For Paul, languages had a place in the faith community only if there was an interpreter. He was concerned about other people and how they would grow and understand the message.

Second, *Paul preferred prophecy*. Prophecy meant "speaking a message," usually God's message. The word in Greek meant "to speak out." Usually the speaker brought a relevant message rather than a prediction of future events. To prophesy did not suggest a message for the distant future; it suggested a message of encouragement. Paul stated that prophecy spoke to people to encourage them (14:3), built up the church (14:4, 12), used the mind and the spirit (14:15), was for unbelievers (14:24), and should be done in turn so that people could understand (14:31).

Paul suggested that prophecy involved teaching people in an understandable way. He wanted the church to encourage each other, not themselves. Paul suggested that languages/tongues were confusing (14:7), unintelligible speech (14:11), foreign to some of the hearers (14:11), unfruitful to the mind (14:14), selfish (14:1–2), and questioned its validity in the assembly (14:6). Paul also stated that languages/tongues were "speaking into the air (14:9), equated with their childish behavior (14:20), and confused outsiders who enter an assembly. Indirectly Paul seemed to ask them to be silent (14:28). However, prophecy encouraged not only the church but outsiders and could bring glory to God because prophecy convicts their hearts. Prophecy was designed for others.

Agape seeks the benefit of others. For Paul tongues/languages in the assembly did not create an environment of love but competition and arrogance. Paul wished to curb this problem and, very diplomatically, asked the church to focus on others. This was to be done through prophecy, interpreting languages, and submission. Spirituality was displayed not by languages, power gifts, and selfishness, but by thinking of others. This is the way of *agape*.

Agape and Relationships

1 COR 14:26–39

What is it, brothers and sisters? When you gather, each has:
- a hymn,
- a lesson,
- a revelation,
- a language,
- or an interpretation.

Let everything be done for building up/encouragement.

If anyone speaks in a language, there should be only two or at the most three (each in turn) and let someone interpret.
> If there is no one to interpret, let them keep silent in church and speak to themselves and to God.

Let two or three prophets speak, and let the others weigh what is said.[1]
> If a revelation is made to another sitting there, let the first be silent. For you can all prophesy one by one, so that all may learn and all be encouraged, and the spirits of prophets are submissive to the prophets.

For God is not a God of confusion but of peace, as in all the churches of the saints

The women should keep silence in the churches because they are not permitted to speak, and should be in submission, as the law also says. If they want to know anything they should ask their

> husbands at home. It is shameful for a woman to speak in church (an assembly).
>
> Was it from you that the word of God came? Or are you the only ones it has reached?
>> If anyone thinks that they are a prophet, or spiritual, they should acknowledge that the things I am writing are a command of the Lord.
>> If anyone does not recognize this, they are not recognized.
>
> So, my brothers and sisters, desire to prophesy, and do not forbid speaking in languages.

The reason that Paul curbed languages/tongues was because it created an atmosphere of power, competition, and selfishness. However, Paul felt that *agape* created an atmosphere of giving, support, caring, and peace. Paul wanted outsiders who entered the assembly to see the church as a place of peace. Since ancient homes existed on small roads, and were places of business, outsiders were easily able to enter the assembly. Those passing by would hear the commotion and may stick their head inside the doorway to see what was happening. Since Sunday was a regular work day for most people (the Sabbath is Saturday and only the Jews would have celebrated that day as a day of rest) customers would have come into the home/shop and visited. Paul was concerned about not only their understanding of worship, but their experience of the assembly. Paul showed concern in these verses:

- 14:16 The group needed to be able to understand and agree with what was said.
- 14:17 Prayers should be in a language that others can understand. They should not put people to sleep. They should encourage.
- 14:17 God has not given us a prayer language. It is to be understood by common people.
- 14:17 Worship is not about power but love/*agape*.
- 14:17 Submission is key to worship. This reflects *agape* (1 Cor. 8–10) and allows people the opportunity to participate.
- 14:23, 33 Outsiders needed to see that the church had order. This was a reflection of God as well.
- 14:27–31 Order was important not only as an appearance but also so that the group could hear, digest, and discuss the message.

- 14:32 Spiritual submission involved self control rather than a lack of control.
- 14:33 Order, not chaos, is the way of God and *agape*. God created the world out of chaos (Gen 1). Chaos was the world of evil.
- 14:34 Women were going to be viewed by the authorities (as well as the *oikonomia*) since they were in the presence of men at the assembly. They were to be protected in the assembly and encouraged to speak at home. Paul, once again, was not putting women in their place but protecting them.

Paul suggested that an orderly worship/assembly not only brought glory to God, it protected the church (especially the women and lower social classes) from outside accusations. As mentioned earlier, some religions in the ancient world manifested chaos, ecstatic language, curses, and fear. These were also selfish religions. Many people joined these movements because they gave the people a sense of power. In some circles, the lower classes were invited to join these groups which gave them a sense of belonging and power. Other religious groups fostered community, support, and acceptance. Those power religions were highly suspect by the political authorities who were in charge of maintaining public order. They were also part of the temporary empire.

Paul focused on the church's reputation as a community of fellowship, love, support, care, kindness, and empowerment. While converts to Christianity brought their views of spirituality into the community Paul reminded them that this community was different. It was a community of love, empowerment, self-sacrifice, encouragement, and ethical behavior. It was a movement seeking to be a resource in the community, not pose a threat. The Christians at Corinth needed to mature and Paul suggested that love/agape would help them in their journey.

Agape as a Way Today

Spiritual maturity today reflects the same love and sacrifice for others that it did two thousand years ago. Christianity has tried to define spirituality through knowledge, advanced education, social status, power, and prestige. However, the church historically has grown when Christians focus on reaching out to the poor, oppressed, and hurting. Sin, however is not limited by class. Too often churches focus on maintaining members or their status in the community. Other churches become compulsive about traditions and are driven by fear of the changing community.

The church of *agape* is driven by love. As the Apostle John wrote:

> "There is no fear in love, but mature love drives fear away. Fear has to do with punishment, and whoever fears is not maturing in love," (1 John 4:18).

Spiritual maturity is not defined by longevity on earth or in the church. It is defined by one's ability and willingness to practice unconditional love. In this case this younger generation may condemn the older. Lori and I were challenged by younger people at Agape to move out of our comfort zones. We decided we would either be leaders who discouraged them and held them back, or leaders who would go ahead of them and walk with them. We also realized that our sons needed to see that mom and dad were not afraid to take risks.

Spiritual maturity is not only manifested in outreach but in building up the church. Early Christian worship was simple. While God is the focus of our praise others, especially visitors, are also the intended recipients of our love. I remember hearing a song suggesting "I seek to worship for an audience of one..." However, Paul suggests that our worship extend to others. The one who had an audience of one was encouraged to keep silent, "But if there is no one to interpret, let them keep silent in church and speak to themselves and to God." Our worship must also manifest this concern for others.

The church should place an emphasis on encouraging Christians, guests to the assembly or small groups, and the surrounding community. This is practiced in sermons, education, and fellowship groups. The message should be clear and easy to understand by all people. It is also one that reflects order rather than chaos. People seeking Jesus are not looking for hype and excitement. They desire something stable, permanent, and mature. Teaching and encouragement draw others closer to Jesus because these gifts reflect *agape* love, support, and caring for others.

Paul challenged the church to keep their worship grounded in love. There were obvious divisions manifested between rich and poor in worship due to hoods, food, neglecting those without, and the practice of "power spirituality." For Paul *agape* love is the manifestation of true spiritual maturity. This *agape* embraces outsiders and the poor and empowers them to have an intimate relationship with God and the community. While the temporary empire may have seen this as stupidity, it is the better way. It lasts and still continues to transform lives today. It is a permanent virtue that stabilized an empire in the midst of the fading realm and vanishing kingdom.

In our ministry to Portland I constantly hear drug and alcohol counselors, abuse advocates, those who help rehabilitate women in the sex industry, and those working with the homeless tell me that one key to healing comes from the faith community and spirituality. I represent the faith communities in Oregon on the Attorney General's Sexual Assault Task Force and find the participants very open to engaging faith communities. Government servants continually share with me that faith communities are important in protecting women and children, and helping men change their violent behavior. They realize that in their realm of power, control, pain, suffering, and violence unconditional love provides hope for human transformation. It also provides hope for justice.

> What an awesome testimony from those who enter our assembly as outsiders.
> What an awesome opportunity for God's people to prophesy and cause others to declare that God is among us.

8

Resurrection Power: Life Sucks, or Does It?

RESURRECTION APATHY

IN THE UNITED STATES we have a tradition. If your life has been questionable and you die, the preacher says nice things about you at the funeral. Sometimes they feel that their role is to either preach the deceased into heaven or avoid talking about judgment, hell, and the throne of God. It is uncommon for funeral attendees to hear the deceased judged for his/her behavior and the congregation warned not to imitate the deceased person's life. George Carlin once wrote,

> Why is it we never hear that someone is "smiling up at us?" I suppose it doesn't occur to people that a loved one might be in hell. And in that case the person in question probably wouldn't be smiling. More likely, he'd be screaming. "I get the feeling he's down there now, screaming up at us. And I think he's in pain." People just refuse to be realistic.[1]

I heard a story about a priest and two brothers who were Mafia leaders. One of the brothers died and the living brother went to take care of the funeral arrangements. He hired the priest to speak and told him, "I will give you one-million dollars to do the funeral." This sounded good to the priest who ministered at a church that was in a poor neighborhood. The brother continued and said, "The only condition is that you call my brother a saint during the service." The priest saw the declining building and realized that this money could help their ministry. However, he had an ethical dilemma: both brothers were evil men. The priest agreed to the conditions.

During the funeral all of the family, friends, enemies, and business associates were present for the funeral service. Many came to pay their

---

1. Carlin, *When Will Jesus Bring the Pork Chops?*, 133.

respects but others came to hear what the priest had to say. The priest began the service and spoke about the brother. He shared how evil and wicked the deceased was and told personal stories of the lives he had crushed. He stood before the family and looked the living brother in the eyes and condemned the deceased's actions, violence, and extortion. The family became angry and the living brother was seething with rage. Then the priest stopped, walked closer to the living brother and said, "While the deceased was an evil man I would have to say that compared to his brother Marcus, he was a saint."

Rarely do we hear people speak out at funerals. It is even rarer that clergy do not preside at funerals. Most people believe in an afterlife and funerals remind us that we are concerned with our faith, purpose, and if God is our judge. In the United States most of us view faith and religion as an important part of the dying and grieving process.

However, this was not true in the ancient world of Corinth. Archaeologists have found that ten per-cent of funeral inscriptions in the Greek and Roman culture "contain even a hint of a hope for an afterlife."[2] The typical views of death were:

- "I did not exist, I came into being, I will not exist anymore. I do not care—that's life."
- "I did not exist, I do not exist, I do not care."
- "I was nothing. I am nothing; and you who [now] live, eat, drink, play, come!"[3]
- 1 Cor. 15:32, "Let's eat and drink because we may die tomorrow."

There was little hope in death. Because of this people saw religions that promised reward in the afterlife as bogus. At Corinth, religions were losing their power and the afterlife was but a myth, at least among those of the upper-class.

1 Cor 15:1–20

> Brothers and sisters, I want you to know about the gospel that I preached to you—the one you embraced which supports you and saves you (assuming that you hold to the message I told you about so that you don't come out of what you believed).

2. Klauck, 80.
3. Ibid.

> The first thing I did was to teach you what I received:
> Jesus died for our sins according to the scriptures
> he was buried
> and he rose on the third day according to the scriptures
> and Cephas saw him
> then the twelve
> then he was seen by more than five hundred brothers and sisters at once,
> many are still alive but some have died.
> Then James
> then again to the apostles
> last of all, as to one born dead, I saw him. I am the least of the apostles; I shouldn't be called an apostle because I persecuted God's church. I am what I am because of God's grace, which was not wasteed on me. I worked harder than any of them, although it was not me, but God's grace within me. Whether it was I or they, you believed what we preached.
>
> If Christ is proclaimed as risen from the dead, how can some of you say that there is no resurrection of the dead?
>> If there is no resurrection of the dead, then Christ has not been raised.
>>> If Christ has not been raised, then our preaching is in empty and your faith is empty.
>>> We are misrepresenting God, because we testified that God raised Christ, whom God did not raise if it is true that the dead are not raised.
>>> If the dead are not raised, not even Christ has been raised.
>>> If Christ has not been raised, your faith is wasted and you are still in your sins.
>> Those also who have died in Christ have perished.
>
> If in this life we have hoped in Christ, we are of all people most to be pitied. But Christ has been raised from the dead, the first fruits of those who have died.

The Corinthian Christians must have wrestled with this issue as well. Paul suggested that their hope of an afterlife lie in the resurrection of Jesus. For Paul a denial of the resurrection was the same as the denial of an afterlife. The Corinthians also believed that Rome would be the source of resurrection. Since Julius Caesar claimed to have resurrected Corinth out of the ashes (44 BCE) the Roman Empire reminded the Corinthians that they were living in the resurrection. Corinth was a new city, a renewed empire, and had a new Lord who was Caesar. Unfortunately, this new life or *oikoumenē*, according to Paul, was transitory. It was passing away, unstable, and incomplete. In their conversion or baptism (6:11; 12:13) into the empire, they had left the fading kingdom for a world of love, empowerment, and maturity. This was expressed in the resurrection of Jesus.

The Resurrection and Transformation

Paul mentioned that the good news/message of Jesus had a transformative quality. Jesus' death, burial, resurrection, and appearing to others not only proved the power of God, it became a path of transformation and initiation into a new realm of existence. This transition happened as they also followed Jesus' example by their death (repentance and self-denial—Luke 9:23), burial (baptism in water—Rom 6:1–6; Col 2:11–12), and resurrection and appearing (personal life and witness in the new kingdom—Rom 6:7–11). Their imitation of this "humiliated Messiah" (1 Cor 1:18–26) had consequences in their social communities. The power of Rome to create a new city was evident in their daily lives. Yet this empire's power was fading. Jesus' empire was present and transforming their lives. The power of Jesus to create new life could only be evident in how they lived their lives, conduct, and works of faith.

The church seemed to have been struggling with the belief in the resurrection of Jesus. First, *Paul used himself as evidence of a resurrection.* In the past, Paul had murdered Christians for their faith. In Acts 9 Paul was a powerful young Pharisee who was a leader in the Jewish community. He felt compelled to oppose Christianity. However, Jesus appeared to him on a mission and blinded him. Paul's refusal to believe, unlike the other apostles and Christians, reminded him of his own humiliation in conversion. He called himself a "still birth," (1 Cor 15:8). In conversion Paul felt out of place, because he had opposed this movement. Jesus also had to make a special appearance to Paul to get his attention and get him on board with his mission. Because of this Paul worked hard and let God's grace transform him. He also believed that this was a display of God's grace. Paul was a testimony that this new kingdom was a place of transformation.

Second, *Paul argued that there was hope in the resurrection.* If people were baptized into Jesus, who they thought hadn't raised from the dead, what good had it done? Paul challenged them to believe that Christianity was not just a "good philosophy," but a faith and transformational kingdom. Greeks questioned the resurrection (Acts 17), and it is possible that many in the church were affected by this belief.[4] However, Paul suggested that if that was true, they were living a powerless life for a powerless lie. The Corinthians needed to understand that the clash of these two empires involved hope in the afterlife.

Finally, *Paul used common agricultural analogies to express the logic of the resurrection.* He suggested that crops, plants, and the skies followed seasons and cycles (15:35–44). The goal of the cycle was to bring a harvest and produce fruit that was vastly different from the seed. This transformation began with the death of the seed but ended with fruit that in turn produced many seeds. The cycle continued. For Paul the resurrection was that final fruit that reflected the growth, transformation, and production of the faith and love of the Christian. However, this could only happen if the Christian was willing to mature in love.

Death was a small but necessary part of this cycle; however it was still a necessary part of this cycle. As in nature, life carries on. As in nature the harvest/judgment manifests the fruit of the growth or life of the individual. For Paul the death and resurrection was a part of this life cycle. Those who lived without hope saw no need for a resurrection. Therefore they saw no need to finish the Christian race. They also would see no need to mature, grow, and sacrifice for others. Throughout the book Paul has encouraged the Christians to grow, develop, mature, and practice love for each other. Paul mentioned that faith, hope, and love remained in the Christian life (13:19; 14:1). However, it was those three virtues, as well as others, that could bring about maturity in the Christian. The Christian who did not believe in the resurrection of Jesus only saw part of the cycle of life. They did not see the joy of the harvest and the hope of transformation.

I find that there are Biblical scholars, ministers, and Christians who do not believe that Jesus resurrected. They see Jesus as a philosopher, a good man, or a prophet. Yet I wonder what hope they have of transformation. According to Paul, belief in a religion initiated by a dead man had

---

4. Anderson, *But God Raised Him from the Dead*, 97–101.

little power. He believed that the resurrection had implications for all that he had written. If Jesus did not raise from the dead then:

- People were baptized into the name of a dead man.
- People were following a man who taught that he was God. He must somehow be wrong.
- People are following centuries of leaders who were also deluded by his teachings.
- We can only focus on his words as good ethical teachings.
- Christianity is based on a deluded man's philosophy.
- Power, transformation, and change are dependent of the value of a teaching, not the power of a divine being.
- This is as good as it gets.
- Christians should be mocked.
- Our hope is a pipe dream, not a real experience.

Paul echoed these statements in 1 Cor 15:29–34. If there were no resurrection, then they were being baptized for a dead man (Jesus). Throughout the letter he suggested that they embrace a permanent empire and reject a fading one. Why? They must do this because the resurrection proved that humiliation and sacrifice brings fruit, transformation, power, and love. The Corinthians lived daily with the reminders that claimed Rome had the power to create, rebuild, and give life. The poor could be crushed or saved by this power. Jesus' crucifixion was the Roman stamp that they had power even to destroy a god. The resurrection of Jesus gave hope to the oppressed that Rome was powerless and that the empire of power was passing away.

Seeing the Resurrection and Transformation

There is an advantage to being a minister. I see transformation in my own life and the lives of others. Those with drug addictions, sexual addictions, self-destructive tendencies, survivors of violence, trauma, abuse, and many others who suffer have shared their faith with me. I ask, "Can a good philosopher transform these people?" When I ask them they tell me the truth.

- Only God not a philosophy
- Only Jesus not a good person
- Only the Spirit not a positive attitude
- Only the resurrection not a religion
- Only a community of those who have been transformed not a social gathering
- Only love not oppression

The Resurrection as Power

The resurrection of Jesus is the central core to the Christian life. While every major religion as well as many historians acknowledges the life and death of Jesus, few accept the resurrection. This distinguishes Christianity from all other belief systems. Yet this resurrection does not mean we are better or more privileged than any other belief. It means that our identity exists based upon our acceptance of the resurrection's truth and continuation in our lives.

First, *embracing the resurrection means that we accept Paul's thesis throughout 1 Corinthians*. Paul presents us with a model of God's transformation and power in this book. God's way is that the humiliated and oppressed, when chosen and transformed, witness God's power and glorify Jesus' ministry. This happens as the resurrection works through our outreach and evangelism in our communities and neighborhoods. We are called to go to the humiliated of society because their transformation proves Jesus' power. We also witness this power by our own transformation. When the empire of love, mercy, and sacrifices stands firm in a world that fades, people have hope in the way of Jesus.

Second, *embracing the resurrection means that we view power differently than the rest of the world*. Like the Corinthians, we live in an empire that sees little need for religion or Christianity. In western culture Christianity is viewed as irrelevant. This happened because we focused on doctrine, proving our worth, or lamenting that we have lost power over our government and local institutions. I hear many Christians in America whine because our public institutions have removed prayer, bible readings, and "God." We feel that we are no longer in power or control. However, we never were in control. We were never meant to be in power. At Corinth, the Christian's power was seen in their practice of love, not control. Love was/is the measure of spiritual maturity. Christianity practices the resurrection when we live as if love, unity, compassion, and mercy are our highest goals. We no longer worry about being in control but in guiding people to transform.

The Resurrection as Transformative Power

Belief in the resurrection means that we accept that transformation is the norm. As Paul mentioned, life is filled with transition. Crops die, grow, transform, bring fruit, and die again. These seeds then continue the cycle again. For the church, transformation and change are expected. Maturity happens when we practice agape. The resurrection of Jesus provides hope that people transform. It also provides a model for the Christian life.

The church is not an institution worth preserving. The church is not a business. The church is not a hospital for sinners. The church is a place where people heal, change, and step into leadership. The church is like a cancer cell—it rapidly grows and affects the tissue around it. It also breaks down tissue in its path. Leaders are called to guide people to transform, mature, develop, and imitate the model of Jesus.

The church must also affect the surrounding community. The presence of Christians means that our communities should be blessed by God. By practicing love and hope our community should "fall down and declare that God is among us" (1 Cor 14:25). Our society should see that we not only uphold a common ethic, but that we are of value to them. We must show our communities that we are a stable presence in a changing world.

Jesus had predicted his death and humiliation at Jerusalem, his burial, and resurrection (Luke 9:21–22). However, it was not until he appeared to the apostles that they began to believe. While those who saw Jesus preached out of knowledge and conviction, this was a valuable component to their faith. Paul was also convinced by Jesus' appearing.

Likewise, the church will never convince people of the power of Jesus until we "appear" to others. Occasionally my friend, who is agnostic and teaches philosophy at a local community college, and I will host discussions/debates with each other or invite the leaders from Portland's United State's Atheists to join the debates. Many of our college students and friends from church enjoy attending these discussions. One year the president of the USAA came to speak. He had worked for NASA and is a very intelligent man. He began his talk with his "Thesis Concerning Faith."

One of the points was that religion serves no value in our society. After the discussion he visited with many of the Christian college students who shared with him the many acts of compassion they provided Portland. Some of them also challenged him about his service to his community. He emailed me the next day and said that he wished to change one of his thesis statements. After the wonderful conversations he had with the kids he decided that "religion does have value in our society." While I have always appreciated the openness and generosity of my friends who hold differing beliefs, I can't help but see that active, compassionate, loving Christians go a long way in convincing people of the life of Jesus.

How Christians appear to their communities will either prove that Jesus is dead or convince people that he lives and moves among us even today. Even more the resurrection is not the final stamp of the faith. Paul reminded the Corinthians that their ministry and service would bring about a fruitful harvest. In 15:58 he suggested that they "give themselves completely to the Lord's work . . ." For Paul, they had hope of an afterlife because of the transformation and healing in their lives. Jesus still lives and his resurrection reminds us that life continues to grow and bear fruit in both this world and the next.

9

Relieving Others

1 Cor 16:1–4

> Concerning the matter/collection for the saints, you are to do as I directed the churches in Galatia.
> On the first day of each week, each of you is to put something aside and store it up, as they are blessed (prosper), so that there will be no collection when I come.
> When I arrive, I will send those whom you approved by letter to carry your gift to Jerusalem. If it is good for me to go, they will accompany me.

IMAGINE WHAT THE SUNDAY worship in Corinth must have looked like. 1 Cor 12–14 suggest that, at times, there was chaos and confusion. These chapters also suggest that people had something to share and that there was a sense of eagerness and joy. Chapter 11 indicated that the Christians ate together but sometimes neglected to share with each other. If you looked around the gathering you would see a diverse group of people. On Sunday you may have seen slaves, owners, wealthy, poor, Jews, Romans, Greeks, Syrians, Asians, men, women, children, public officials, soldiers, and common people. The first century church was quite diverse both ethnically and economically. We do not know how large the church was but it could have been any size from forty to a larger sized group.[1]

---

1. de Vos suggests that the church could have been over 40 people (203), while Osiek and Balch suggest that many homes would allow 60–360 people in attendance (201–04). They even claim that there were rare occasions where a home could hold 1200 people. "The need for all early Christian assemblies to have been small and private is a modern projection, not justified by Roman domestic culture or architecture." Oseik and Balch, 201–3. Paul named the household of Stephanus (16:15), Chloe (1:10), and Gaius (Paul's

To this group Paul decided to formulate a plan to financially support God's people in other locations. This contribution was not for the Corinthian church, but another group of Christians who needed help. In Acts 11:27–28 the prophet Agabas predicted a famine in Jerusalem (about 45 CE). The Nile river flooded its banks in Egypt in 45–46 CE which destroyed the grain harvest. Since Egypt was the breadbasket of the Roman Empire the entire Roman world was affected by this food shortage. Cities outside the immediate area of Rome were hit hardest. The farther out one ventured from Rome the more that the food became expensive and in demand.

There were many famines in the Roman world after 48 CE including the wealthy town of Corinth. One famine was so severe that the Isthmian Games had to be returned to their original location after being in Corinth for a century.[2] *Famines* affected the early Christians not only personally, but in their outreach.[3] Famines and other natural disasters also gave the early church opportunities to reach out to those who were hurting. *Disease* was a major problem in the first century. Health care was expensive, if one could afford it. Doctors were usually slaves who were skilled with various forms of magic or medicine. Most of these doctors were located in large cities. Healing cults wee also located in urban areas. Doctors and priests did not make house calls—one had to go to them. Archaeologists have uncovered barracks attached to temples designed to house patients, family, and other attendants but these were usually crowded, especially during seasons of sickness or festivals. Priests traveled extensively and were present in temples in the small cities for a short time. A trip to the doctor could be expensive, take weeks, and be risky. In addition, most people were never cured.

Persecution also became an issue for Christians. While empire-wide persecutions were rare, most Christians faced small family and local attacks caused by local trigger events. Since most people's family life and occupation were blended with idolatry becoming a Christian was risky. Being part of an association or guild required loyalty to a god or goddess. To abandon all idols for Jesus sometimes meant rejection or persecution from family, friends, co-workers, and neighborhoods. It is also likely that

---

host as well as the whole church, Rom 16:23) which may suggest that the church met in multiple locations.

2. Winter, *After Paul Left Corinth*, xi, 6.
3. Hector Avalos, *Health Care*.

Christians (as well as others) could have been blamed for famines and diseases in a community that saw this as a curse from the gods.

The early church focused on helping people in need. Christians adopted abandoned children, healed the sick, fed and clothed the poor, and protected the outcasts and oppressed. Christians were also victims of famine, persecution, and disease and needed to help each other. Clement of Rome once wrote that some Christians sold themselves into slavery to pay off the debts of other Christians or slaves.[4] This ministry, however, required money.

Paul's desire was to provide relief for Christians in other parts of the country. His desire was also that the Christians in the Greek world (Macedonia and Achaia) fund his ministry to others. He wanted the Jewish Christians to see God's work in the Gentiles through their giving and sacrifice of love. In the ancient world this also communicated fellowship (communion), friendship, and kinship. The early mission team believed that these acts of love would strengthen Christian relationships worldwide.

Paul left us hints in his letters that the Greek churches were financially involved in his ministry The Philippian churches shared or partnered with him in his ministry:

> . . . because of your partnership in the gospel from the first day until now. [6] I am sure of this, the one who started a good work in you will complete it at the day of Jesus Christ. (Phil 1:5–6)
>
> I rejoiced in the Lord greatly that you have revived your concern for me. You were really concerned for me, but you had no opportunity (to help).
>
> I am not speaking of being in need, because I have learned in whatever situation I am to be content. I know how to be humiliated, and I know how to abound. In any and every circumstance, I have learned the secret of being content in every situation (well fed or hungry—having plenty and being without). I can do everything through the one who gives me strength.
>
> It was kind of you to share my trouble.
>
> You Philippians know that in the beginning of the gospel, when I left Macedonia, you were the only church to partner with me in giving and receiving.
>
> Even in Thessalonica you sent me help for my needs once and again.

---

4. *1 Clement*, 55.2.

> I don't seek the gift, but I seek the fruit that increases to your credit. I have received full payment, and more. I am well supplied, having received from Epaphroditus the gifts you sent, a fragrant offering, a sacrifice acceptable and pleasing to God.
>
> My God will supply every need of yours according to his riches in glory in Christ Jesus. (Phil 4:10–19)

The Philippian church financially supported Paul's early work in Thessalonica, Berea, Athens, and Corinth (Acts 16–18). From the language in the above texts, Paul suggested that the financial support was a "sharing" in his ministry. This may be why Paul and Silas did not receive support from the Corinthian church while in the city (1 Cor 9:6).

Paul and the team wrote to the Thessalonian church that they were funded by the Philippian church as well as their own personal income. They worked hard and did not expect the Thessalonian church to financially support them while they were there.

> Now we command you, brothers, in the name of our Lord Jesus Christ that you keep away from any brother (or sister) who is idle and not in line with the tradition that you received from us.
> You know how you ought to imitate us, because we were not idle when we were with you, nor did we eat anyone's bread without paying for it, but with hard work and labor we worked night and day, that we might not be a burden to any of you. It was not because we do not have that right, but to give you an example to imitate.
> When we were with you, we would give you this command: If anyone is not willing to work, let them not eat. (2 Thess 3:6–15)

The Thessalonians also displayed their love by supporting Paul, Silas, and the mission team.

> Now concerning love of the family we don't need to write to you, for you have been taught by God to love one another, for that is what you are doing to all the brothers and sisters throughout Macedonia.
> We urge you to do more of this. (1 Thess. 4:9–10)

> I want you to know about the grace of God that has been given to the churches of Macedonia.
> In a severe test of suffering, their abundance of joy and their extreme poverty have overflowed in a wealth of generosity on their

part. They gave according to their means, as I can testify, and
beyond their means, of their own free will, begging us for the
favor of sharing in the relief of the saints.

Not as we expected, but they gave themselves first to the Lord and
then by the will of God to us. (2 Corinthians 8:1–5)

The Macedonian churches funded Paul's mission trip into Achaia and were also involved in financially supporting Paul's relief efforts to other places. The Corinthian church had been the first to offer help to Paul's effort. It seems that Paul had plans, after his trip to Ephesus (Acts 19) to go to Jerusalem and offer this relief to the Jews. Before his work in Ephesus he returned through Galatia, Macedonia, and Achaia (Acts 18:23) to gather financial support for this ministry. Paul viewed this financial gift for the Jews in need as a testimony that God was working among the Gentiles. Paul also felt called to gather a larger collection from the Greek churches in order to provide aid to churches either in Asia or Palestine. While Paul praised the church for this act of love, he wanted them to meet their goal.

Paul compared the Macedonian Christians and the Corinthian Christians in their eager effort to support his ministry. The Corinthian church obviously had many more wealthy individuals than the Macedonian congregations, yet Paul praised the Macedonian churches for their willingness to give without having the financial resources.

We urged Titus that as he had started, so he should finish this act
of grace in your midst.
As you excel in everything
in faith
in speech
in knowledge
in all earnestness,
and in our love for you
make sure that *you excel in this act of grace also.*
I say this not as a command, but to prove that your love is real.
For you know the grace of our Lord Jesus Christ that though he
was rich, yet for your sake he became poor, so that you, by his
poverty/humiliation might become rich.
In this matter I give my judgment: this benefits you, *who a year ago
started to do this work but also wanted to do it.*
*Finish doing it as well, so that your desire it may be matched by your
completing it out of what you have.* (2 Cor 8:6–11)

The Corinthian church eagerly stepped up to lead in this ministry of giving. They had greater financial resources and obviously members with money who could sustain Paul's mission work. Their commitment empowered Paul to set goals and plans for a ministry of support and giving to Christians in other parts of the country. Titus was sent to help the church fulfill their commitment to this ministry.

Somehow the church had fallen behind in their support, or neglected this ministry and Paul encouraged them complete this task. It is possible that the ones who had informed Paul of the issues, mentioned that the church was struggling with included this giving (1 Cor 16:1). Paul used Jesus' ministry as a model for their work. Jesus became poor so that we might be blessed. In turn they were to give back and bless God for this gift.

For Paul this was evidence of God's transformation in the Gentile churches. These churches were giving to a ministry that would help Jewish Christians in their homeland and prove to them that God was working among the Gentiles. This was not just a relief ministry. It was a ministry that proved God had transformed lives. It was a ministry that would illustrate that the Gentiles and Jews were united in the body of Christ.

Paul also believed that relief efforts and financial blessings were proof that God was at work. Giving is not just something we do for a church; it is something we do to prove that God is working in us.

Titus and a brother were sent to Corinth to encourage them to finish their work (2 Cor 8:16–24). Paul emphasized that the church's giving was proof of their love for God and other Christians. Paul wanted to see the church fulfill their commitment; not only to support this work but to prove that the "immoral Gentiles" had been transformed by the Gospel.

> I thought it necessary to urge the brothers to go on ahead to you and arrange in advance *for the gift you have promised, so that it may be ready as a willing gift, not as a forced contribution.* (2 Cor 9:5)

The Corinthians had set the pace for other churches by offering to give to this relief effort. Obviously this motivated the other churches to give. They eventually gave beyond their ability, yet Paul challenged the Corinthians to fulfill their original pledge. For some reason the Corinthians were slacking off in their effort.

> The point is this: whoever is stingy when they sow seed will reap sparingly, and whoever sows generously will also reap bountifully.
> Each one must give as they have made up their mind, not reluctantly or under compulsion, for God loves a cheerful giver.
> God is able to make all grace abound in you, so that you will be sufficient in all things at all times, and you may blessed in every good work.
> As it is written, "He has distributed freely, he has given to the poor; his righteousness endures forever." (2 Cor 9:6–10)

Paul wanted to motivate the church to give, through *agape* rather than force and manipulation. However he encouraged them to give out of:

- Love for God, Paul, and others
- Trust that this ministry would help others and bring glory to God
- God's abundance which is a blessing for both the giver and receiver
- Realization that this was proof of God's power and love working within us.

Why Do We Give Financially Today?

In many churches a collection is taken every Sunday morning. While people tend to complain that churches "talk about giving" it is important to provide people the opportunity to give. Weekly giving was instituted by Paul to help the church reach their goal.

- Paul wanted a weekly contribution to be taken so that those who were blessed would have an opportunity to give
- Paul did not expect people to feel compelled to give
- Paul knew that the weekly contribution would help them reach their financial goal
- Paul illustrated that financial giving empowered God's ministry

Often I hear people complain about giving financially to a church. I know that many ministers hate preaching about giving. We know that someone will be visiting that day who will say, "Every time I go to church they ask for money." Our response is that we don't talk about it. Therefore Christians do not learn that giving and ministry go hand in hand.

Paul was not ashamed to both ask for money and challenge the church to fulfill their obligation. In 1 Cor 16:1–4 Paul empowered the church to help his ministry. *First, the collection was a way to offer people who were blessed the opportunity to give to God.* We should take up a collection each Sunday so that those who have been blessed can give to support ministry. While I believe that churches need to provide for their local needs, part of the budget must include global and benevolence ministries. Weekly contributions provide churches with an opportunity to set aside financially, however tithing and guilt are both foreign to Paul's request in the church. The way of *agape* encourages giving out of love and generosity.

The text does not tell us we have to give each week. The text tells us to take up a collection each week and provide opportunity for giving. This text also refers to a special goal of global benevolence, not just the expenses of the local church. I have listened to people express guilt because they are paid monthly, have little money some weeks, or struggle with tremendous debt. As the collection plate passes by they either increase their guilt by not giving that day, or increase their debt by giving out of compulsion.

This is not God's way. Paul reminded the early church that we are to give as we have been blessed, not out of guilt or force. "God loves a cheerful giver," was Paul's encouragement to the church. Giving is by grace and joy, as God also gave willingly for us. *One emphasis of weekly giving is opportunity, not guilt.*

Second, notice that "tithing," "ten-percent," or "budget," are terms absent from the text. Even though the word "set aside" is similar to "tithe" it is not the same idea. Typically churches use ten-percent as a guide but this comes from what has been called the Old Testament (Lev 27:30; Deut 12:17; Mal 3:6–8). It was also only one of the measures of giving that the Jews had to perform. Temple taxes, sacrifices, and providing for the poor were additional ways that they gave.

Ten-percent in Corinth would not have provided for Paul's ministry. Slaves had little to give. The burden to support the church fell on the wealthy and they would have given more than ten-percent. Those who barely made enough to set aside for their families would also have been expected to help in this contribution. The point of giving is that the church needs to have the opportunity to support ministry financially.

Third, ministries must be up front and honest about the needs of ministry and the goals/vision of the leaders. Leaders set goals and communicate God's vision to people. Leaders must inform members how giving and vision/mission work together. The people then support this vision financially. If the vision is too expensive, the people either respond or encourage the leaders to review and rethink more efficient ways to fulfill the vision. Leaders work with the church to fulfill ministry and engage members in this work.

Fourth, leaders must constantly use the language of sharing and participation with members. The financial empowerment happens when members give from their blessings to help churches minister to others. Ministry takes money, giving, and partners.

Finally, we must acknowledge that churches, ministry, and missions take money. Weekly contributions provide salaries for ministers, missionaries, and staff to live comfortably and provide for themselves and their families. While Paul gave up this right he supported the rights of other ministers to be financially supported. Contributions allow churches to feed the poor, provide relief for those suffering, and empower people in need to be independent. Contributions helped the church become an example in the community by paying the "bills." There is no witness in a church whose ministers live below the poverty level, which cannot help others, and which is in debt to community vendors. Giving helps the church do the ministry that God has called us to do.

As a church that works with many needs I have found that communicating mission and finances has been an important method to helping a congregation give to help others. It is exciting seeing our members who have been homeless, are homeless, or have finally begun to stand on their own give money to help the District Attorney's office provide food for a woman leaving prostitution, help Touch A Life Ministries in Ghana provide fresh water for children and free them from slavery, or donate shoes to a country needing these items. It is even more exciting to see them give back to our sponsoring church in Oklahoma for their annual mission contribution. A sign of spiritual maturity is the practice of love by supporting others financially.

Our finance team works hard to help a small amount of money provide aid to many people. On any Sunday morning at Agape a line of people coming from the street makes their requests known to God, myself, and our finance team. One Sunday the team ran out of benevolence money and told a man, who had been sitting through services, that they had nothing for him. Most people seeking financial assistance have this problem. They wait, and wait, and tell their story over and over again, and sometimes receive nothing.

Upon hearing that there was nothing the man exploded and began to curse at the women on our team. He left in anger. My first thought was to get in his face and not let him come back. As I met with the team they were concerned about the man. They felt that they had hurt him by expecting him to sit through church only to be rejected. I was impressed by the heart of the team. A prayer ministry was developed to receive financial requests, pray with the people, and accompany them throughout the service. We began this ministry the next week. The following happened:

- More adults took part in praying and ministering to our guests with requests
- Financial requests decreased because people felt as if they were being heard
- Our finance team felt less stressed
- I was less stressed
- The man returned weeks later, apologized to the women on the team, and confessed to the church his sin

Agape truly is a better way.

Relieving Those At Corinth

16:5–18

> I will visit you after passing through Macedonia, for I intend to pass through Macedonia, maybe I will stay with you or spend the winter, so that you may help/send me on my journey, wherever I go.
>> I do not want to blow into town and have a quick visit.
>> I want to spend some time with you, if the Lord permits.
>> I will stay in Ephesus until Pentecost, because a door for great work has been opened for me, and there are many opponents.
>
> When Timothy comes, make him feel welcome because he is doing the work of the Lord, just like I am. Don't let anyone one mistreat him. Help him on his way in peace, so that he may return to me, for I am expecting him with the brothers.

> Concerning our brother Apollos, I encouraged him to visit you with the other brothers, but he didn't want to come yet. He will come when he has opportunity.
> Be careful,
> stand firm in the faith,
> act like men [act like adults],
> hang in there.
> do what you do out of *agape*/love!
>
> Now I urge you, brothers and sisters, you know that those in Stephanas' family were the first converts in Achaia, and that they have devoted themselves to the ministry for the saints. Submit/respect people like them and those who work with you and labor.
>
> I was happy when Stephanas and Fortunatus and Achaicus came, because they have made up for your absence and they refreshed my spirit as well as yours.

Paul was planning to leave Ephesus and travel through Greece to gather the collection. He would come to Corinth and relieve them by spending time with them. His trip would begin in Macedonia and then he would travel to Corinth, where he would stay three months (Acts 20:2). Paul wanted to stay in the city and develop relationships with the church, however he will request more support for this trip (16:6).

Paul was concerned about two of his friends who were going to visit Corinth, Timothy and Apollos. For some reason Apollos did not want to go to Corinth but Paul encouraged him to go. Is it possible that Apollos was frustrated that they had been divided over loyalties to him (3:4)? Paul reminded the church to love others (16:14). Paul finished this letter with a reminder that the greatest virtue needed to be practiced in their Christian life.

- Be careful
- Stand firm
- Have courage/act like men or adults
- Hang in there
- Do everything with *agape*

The first four words are military terms. However, Paul believed that *agape* was a central value for the church and needed to be a virtue for this spiritual army. As mentioned earlier he used this world heavily in chapter thirteen. Acting in love (*agape*) takes courage and strength. Acting in love cultivates unity and teamwork. Acting in love is how we stand firm.

God's strength was shown by faithfulness, love, and mercy. God's nature was to love and be faithful in a relationship with us. While we may fail in that relationship we know that God will not be unfair and unfaithful (Tit 1:2). God was not only faithful to the covenant or promise of relationship with Israel, God willingly re-united with them even after they broke the relationship (Deut 7:6–11; Hos 2:14–23). As they returned to God, they were forgiven and re-married to *Yahweh*. While many other gods in the ancient world displayed power and control, *Yahweh* displayed power through love, faithfulness, forgiveness, and mercy. These qualities of God, Paul suggests, display courage and strength. God, the warrior, is a warrior of love. Christians must also display this type of power.

Paul was also concerned that those who had displayed leadership and had worked hard in the faith would not be respected. Timothy, Titus, Apollos, and the messengers from Chloe's house (Fortunatus, and Achaicus) were to be honored and respected. Paul reminds us that how we treat leaders in our churches is a reflection of our own faithfulness in the empire. This does not suggest that we blindly follow leaders nor do we ignore their sin. To the contrary, it means that our leaders who are reputable should be able to do their job because God's people co-operate. As mentioned in 1 Cor 1–4, the church had become contentious over their leaders. Paul first called the Corinthian church to focus on the power of the Gospel, not the person teaching it. In 1 Cor 16, Paul reminded the church that those leaders who model the nature of Jesus (and Paul) should be supported in their ministry.

A MINISTRY OF AGAPE

While this letter reflects Paul's love and concern for the church, it also display's his leadership skills in the empire of Jesus. Paul as a leader ends this letter challenging the church to support his ministry to the poor and lead with *agape*. This *agape* produces maturity in the Christian, but it also transforms Jesus' people to effectively lead in their communities. Leaders in churches must manifest this *agape* in their ministry.

- Leaders must reflect the *agape* of God, Jesus, the Spirit, and the church found in this letter

- Leaders must be people who are moral and who have victories over the sins mentioned in 1 Corinthians (as well as other places in the bible).
- Leaders must display courage, faith, and strength by their practice of *agape* (1 Cor 13).
- Leaders are gifted by the Spirit and fulfill a role in the body of Christ.
- Those leaders who are married must have healthy relationships and family lives. Those who are not should show self-control over sexual issues.
- Leaders are approachable.
- Leaders care about others in the body of Christ and outside the body.
- These leaders have emerged from the church and are worthy of recognition (16:18).

For Paul, Christian leaders set the example and pace for the church in their work and conduct. Leaders who share their faith develop congregations which, in turn, share their faith. Leaders who develop healthy relationships with outsiders and people who do not know Jesus develop members who do the same. Leaders who overcome sin and rise above dysfunction develop members who also rise above sin. Paul also presents a message to the modern church as well.

- We must support, honor, and respect these leaders so that they can do their jobs and fulfill their giftedness.
- We must realize that leaders become responsible for themselves, their families, and others in the church—including you.
- We must support leaders as they confront sin and help people heal.
- We must be committed to the Gospel and message of the kingdom. God has called us to spiritual and numerical growth and we need leaders to set the pace.
- We must be open to our calling to lead so that we can help leaders fulfill their calling
- We must not be afraid to call leaders to holiness and confront those who sin and do not move forward.

The church is a kingdom/empire, with Jesus as king, but also a democracy. Leaders are called to persuade people to follow Jesus the king and they cannot use force to do this. We all work together to spread the empire of God.

After spending two decades in the traditional churches I found that leadership in a church plant is much different. I am a member in the churches of Christ which believe that the minister is not the pastor. Elders are pastors and are supposed to shepherd the flock and work with the minister/evangelist. However, in many of our churches there exists a power struggle between elders and ministers. Unfortunately the ministers in most of our congregations are not able to cast the vision, lead the church to evangelism, and use the authority given to evangelists (1 Tim; 2 Tim; Titus). Because of this many of our ministers have become pastors, hospice chaplains, servants, and focus their ministries inward toward their congregations and to keeping peace and politics in the church. In response, many of our schools are training ministers to be pastors, visit the sick, and produce encouraging sermons.

As a church planter I find that ministry is much different. Leadership and leadership development are key components to this work. Being a minister/evangelist to the community is our calling (rather than focusing solely on the church). This provides opportunity to cast vision, engage the community, and confront the power structures of our *oikoumenē*. This also requires leaders to be moral, compassionate, and courageous. In turn I have noticed that those who claim Jesus as Lord as well as those who don't are willing to support, follow, and be mentored by strong leaders who model the way of *agape*. This is why I believe that Christianity must invest resources into starting new churches in the *oikoumenē*.

Closing Thoughts

16:19-24

> The churches of Asia send you greetings.
> Aquila and Prisca, together with the church in their house, send you greetings in the Lord.
> All the brothers and sisters send you greetings.
> Greet each another with a holy kiss.
> I, Paul, write this greeting with my own hand. If anyone doesn't love the Lord, Lord, let them be cursed.
> May our Lord, come! (Marana tha)

> The grace of the Lord Jesus be with you.
> My love be with you all in Christ Jesus. Amen.

Paul ended this letter with greetings from his friends. Aquila and Priscilla were some of the founding people in the church at Corinth's history. Paul met them, stayed with them, and worked with them making tents (Acts 18). They were Jews who lived at Rome but were kicked out, along with thousands of other Jews, by the Emperor Claudius (49 CE). Obviously they were somewhat wealthy and were able to establish a business. They were also involved with teaching Apollos the Jew (Acts 18:18–28).

After Claudius died many of the Jews returned to Rome. Priscilla and Aquila would have returned and had a church meet in their house. They and the Corinthian Chrisitans would have had fond memories. Paul reminded the church (as he did in 14:37) to listen to him and love God. To not love God would mean a curse. Paul used the Aramaic phrase *marana tha* which means "come Lord." While some see this as a plea for Jesus to return and take them home—it is a curse on people who do not love God.

First, the Day of the Lord (Yom Yahweh) was a dark and scary day for those who were evil. It was a day of judgment. It occurred many times in scripture and there were many days of the Lord (Joel 1:15). It was a day when God (*Yahweh*) would tear open the heavens and come to earth (usually riding the clouds—Is 19:1–4). The imagery here was common in the ancient world where the Canaanite god, Baal, was the one who "rides the clouds." The coming of Yahweh was similar to mom or dad standing at the bottom of the stairs, at nine-o'clock in the evening, and hollering up to my brother and I (who were supposed to be asleep), "Don't make me come up there." This statement never brought joy to us, unless my little brother felt oppressed. "The coming" of our parents, meant relief if you were suffering but fear if you were disobedient.

The coming of God and Day of the Lord were God's interventions in time and space. It was God's presence, visitation, and judgment. *Second, those who saw the coming were the ones being punished.* When Jesus said that he would "come on the clouds" to judge Jerusalem (Matt 24; Mark 13: Luke 21) the ones who would see this (called they in the texts) were the wicked. The coming of Jesus was a curse on the wicked and sometimes vindication for the suffering.

When Paul wrote *marana tha* in 1 Cor 16:22 he was in essence saying, "For those of you who do not love the Lord—God will deal with you. The grace of the Lord Jesus help you." It was a sobering thought for the ancient church as well as the church today. We do not judge, God judges (5:13). We love and ask Jesus' grace to intervene. However, God will intervene in good time. Those who refuse to follow the way of *agape* will stand before God but we continue to practice love, compassion, and acceptance.

It is fitting that Paul ends the letter by appealing to *agape* three times. He encourages them to do everything in love (16:14), let God curse those who do not love (16:22), and receive his love (16:24). For Paul *agape* is the permanent force in the empire of Jesus. Therefore, it should be a major focus for the church and its leaders. While Paul challenged them to love he gave them his love in the last sentence of the letter.

Ending our conversations with "I love you," "Love you," "Love yah man," or "Give my love to . . ." are heartfelt expressions when shared with those we know and love. Sometimes we accidentally sign off by saying, "Love you—ooops," and smile or laugh because of the mistake. However, people understand and maybe for a brief moment hope that the sentiment is true. One of our men who attends Agape and is a member of a homeless community in our ministry was talking with me on the phone the other day. His family had lost a baby to SIDS and we were planning out the funeral. As he was hanging up he said, "OK, love you . . ." to which I hesitated, then smiled and said, "Uh—yah—yes, I love you too."

I was struck by that fact that I have spent years as a white middle class male who, until recently, felt people made their own beds and could pull themselves up by their own bootstraps. The limits of my compassion were in opening my wallet to give out money only to walk away and leave the problem behind me. Since God, and our young people, have been teaching me *agape* I have learned that I was the one with the problem. I had the problem of saying "I love you . . ." first. I had the problem of withdrawing my hand and withholding love from those who needed it. I was the one who developed the wrong target group. I was the one who had forgotten that Jesus called the oppressed long before he called me. I was the one who needed to hear "I love you . . ." from a guy who understood grace more than I ever will.

> Maybe one day I may be the first to say, "My love to all of you in Christ Jesus." Maybe one day I won't hesitate when one in God's image says it to me.

10

Revisiting Corinth

WHEN I BEGAN PREACHING this book at Agape I never realized how powerful the messages were to those struggling with life, sin, and their walk with Jesus. As I read and studied as many resources as I could find on Corinth and the early church I became fascinated with the city, the apostle, and the church. Our three month sermon series became a three month journey into an ancient culture. Yet we constantly talked in the present because we never left the city of Portland. However, I have moved on to other sermons, writings, and facets of the ministry at Agape. I walked down the jetway and flew out of the world of Corinthians and on to other destinations.

The people at Agape regularly talk about the book. I hear that some are reading it again, with a new perspective. Others are studying some of the texts a little deeper. More are using the stories and scriptures in their walk with God. It is cool hearing stories from our three month trip and listening to people share their memories. At times, when I am asked to speak at another church, I preach about the "better way" and overview the book. It is like watching old movies from my vacation to Corinth. Other times it is like revisiting the city with a new group of people.

RETURN TO CORINTH

Paul's letter to the Corinthians has tremendous application for the modern church. The church of the twenty-first century is similar to the church at Corinth. While two-thousand years separate our churches the implications are the same. We, like the Corinthian Christians, are emerging. The churches in the US, Canada, and Europe are struggling to grow and regain the influence that we have had for centuries. While the church is exploding in China, Africa, South America, and Indonesia we are learning that the Gospel provides peace to those who live in poverty, persecution, and powerlessness. We who reside in the cultures of power find ourselves caught in the clash of empires. The empire of Jesus collides with the temporary, fading, and violent empire of modern day Rome. It seems odd that the permanent reality struggles with that which is imperfect and is passing away. This happens because it seems that *agape* has lost its way in our culture. *Agape* is the better way, maturity, and empowering but it only takes effect in lives willing to submit to the Lord Jesus. Unfortunately, many of us are so enamored by the temporary we forget that there is a better way. Might I suggest we don't long for a better way?

Yet 1 Corinthians still holds the key to the return of this empire. Paul's life and letter can guide us as we return to Corinth, gather memories and souvenirs, and build a new empire. Yet we must begin with the belief that Jesus established this empire.

In the Gospels Jesus claimed to bring a new kingdom/empire. In Mark 1:15 he said that the empire was near. He later told a lawyer that he was "not far from the empire . . ." (12:34). I don't believe that Jesus was telling the people that the kingdom was near chronologically (it is coming sometime soon) but spatially (it is present but in a different realm). He said this while people lived under the Roman Empire. However, he told the governor Pilate that the empire was from above and not of this world (John 18:36). The empire of Jesus was and is a present kingdom in the midst of other empires. Jesus reigns even during the reign of worldly leaders. When the Jews were taken captive to Babylon and saw the power struggles of political kingdoms such as Babylon, Persia, and Greece, Daniel mentioned that God's kingdom was permanent and stronger than the political/earthly empires (Dan 2:44). Those suffering and longing for salvation were reminded that God's kingdom still existed, even though a human empire seemed to be in control. They were also reminded that God's empire was eternal and would outlive any other kingdom.

Today we preach a present empire, an alternate reality, and a new world of love and peace. This empire exists alongside any other empire on earth. The people who live on this earth and in the temporary kingdom are called to open their eyes to this new empire and embrace the movement. We do this through belief, repentance, and baptism—or as Jesus suggests, "unless one is born again [from above] they cannot see the empire of God . . . unless one is born of water and the Spirit they cannot enter the kingdom of God," (John 3:3, 5). Through this conversion we pass through a portal to the new empire of *agape* which is the permanent, stable, and mature empire. Paul refers to this as being "transferred from the empire of darkness to the empire of God's loved son . . ." (Col 1:13).

The Permanent Empire

Paul throughout this letter contrasts the fading empire of Rome with the permanent empire of Jesus. Rome had rebuilt Corinth as a Roman city. Rome governed Corinth with Roman rule. Rome transformed Corinth with Roman culture. Power, violence, exploitation, and class distinctions were the fabric of this empire and drove the *oikoumenē*. Yet Paul reminds us that this empire and its view of reality are being abolished (1:28; 2:6; 2:14; 7:31; 13:8). The empire was passing away and fading in its glory. The glory of Rome was only the glory of humans. This realm was divisive, immature, and self centered. It was not destined to be. It could not last. It was human.

However, the empire of Jesus and *agape* were permanent. *Agape* is the better way. *Agape* is maturity, endures, is the greatest, and drives this realm. *Agape* seeks the benefit of others, sacrifices for the week, and reflects the humiliation and vulnerability of a God who loves us enough to die for us, even the shameful and humiliating death on a cross. Jesus died so that the humiliated and oppressed of society could have hope. Even more, Jesus chose the oppressed so that they could glorify God's love and power.

Today, the empire of *agape* exists alongside the *oikoumenē*. *Agape* is the better way. *Agape* is maturity. *Agape* heals, endures, and transforms. *Agape* drives the empire of Jesus in the realm that values power, oppression, and exploitation. *Agape*, however, always wins.

The Leader of Agape

While Paul has been a controversial figure in our history, no one can deny his passion for ministry. Paul, the converted Jewish rabbi was sent by God to the wicked and immoral city of Corinth. Paul would have worked with his hands in the tent shop, slept on the cold floor, and eaten with those outside his ethnic group. Paul faced persecution for his faith and was rejected by his own ethnic group. However, in the silence and loneliness of Corinth God told him that Jesus' people were in the city. Gentiles who did not know the one true God were God's people and Paul found them. This was not his target group but they were his children.

Paul took ownership with these people who needed guidance, support, and encouragement. He claimed to be their patron, father, fellow worker, and asked them to imitate his life for Jesus. Paul was not afraid to be personal with people. Paul was not afraid to move among the people. Paul was not afraid to take the teachings of Jesus to the poor, oppressed, and sinful. Paul modeled discipleship, called them to a better life, and encouraged them to transform. Paul was not afraid to develop relationships with people outside his comfort zones. He, like Jesus, was a friend of sinners and tax collectors.

The churches in North America face a dilemma. Even more we have a leadership crisis. I have taught at seminary, Bible College, and at conferences. I am scared for the future of the church. I see who we have as leaders. I know many of the young men entering ministry. Some avoid those outside the church and in the community. Some stay in the office and prepare or research their sermons. Some refuse to preach on the issues of abuse and exploitation that happen in our society. Others work hard to keep outsiders outside the empire of Jesus. Many continue to objectify women, struggle with pornography, and hide personal sins. I fear that many of these men would wet their pants if they ever had to take the Gospel to Jesus' target group—the oppressed, abused, and marginalized. Even worse, many of our conferences and conventions hold these ministers up as our model of ministry. Yet we never address the problems we face as a declining church. Our young people leave because they do not see courage in the church, only convenience.

Our churches suffer for this. Our members are numb. They don't know the vision of the community of Jesus why they continue to come. They enter the assembly and are given spiritual valium. "Here, take this, swallow it, and you will go numb. Then everything will be OK." Our leaders become pill pushers rather than shepherds. We hold back the ones who want to cast vision, hope, and drive toward the empire of Jesus. They either leave or succumb to our pill pushing ways. Our target group is not Jesus' target group. Very few of us can say, ". . . and such were some of you . . ." or ". . . not many of you were noble, not many of you were wise . . ." because we look the same, we think the same, and we fade in and out like the temporary world that has affected our churches.

> I have seen it in the sad and tired eyes of ministers, their wives, church members, and even worse, the young people. The fire that burned within them has faded, just like the temporary empire.

We need leaders similar to Paul. We need people who take risks. We need to encourage those with vision and passion to lead. We need to listen to them and follow those who model Christ. We need to find opportunities to let them go. We need to support them and encourage them to believe that *agape* changes everything it touches. We need to send them over the sea. Even more, we need to send them to the US, the largest unchurched country in the world. We need to empower them to lead new churches and pray that they say "no" to spiritual valium and "yes" to spiritual maturity. We need to identify our young people who live by vision, faith, and love and guide them to lead in the permanent empire of Jesus. Even more than this, those of us who are older need to repent, go through spiritual drug rehab, and recover from this addiction of spiritual valium and fear. We need to step up and lead. We need to say, "Imitate me as I imitate Christ," because we know that *agape* is the better way.

Resetting the Agape Button

Finally, we need to use the reset button with those seeking the empire of Jesus. God has not called us to condemn or fight with each other. God has called us to be like Paul and sacrifice to "win as many as possible." People who are enslaved in this fading empire need to know that they are the body of Jesus, bought by Jesus, loved by God, and called into the empire of *agape*. The empire of power destroys hope and discourages those who feel that change is not possible. However, the empire of *agape* provides hope, love, and courage. Sine God believes that people can say no to sin (1 Cor 10:13), we must provide this hope and wisdom to others. Seeing God face to face is not the result of a ritual, it is the fruit of loving Jesus and others.

> In a fading world *agape* shines brightly.
> In a temporary empire love remains.
> In an oppressive realm Jesus calls, chooses, and empowers.
> Only when we "do everything in love." (1 Cor 16:14)

In a world that sees its deity as an enigma through a warped mirror we need to introduce them to a God who loves them. We need to show them *agape* so that they can see God face to face, mouth to mouth, eye to eye, and friend to friend. We can lead them to transformation, rather than judgment. We can show them something permanent, something stable, something marvelous. We can show them *agape* so that they can fall to their faces and once again say, "God is truly among you."

Bibliography

Anderson, Kevin L. *"But God Raised Him From the Dead," The Theology of Jesus' Resurrection in Luke-Acts*. Waynesboro, GA: Paternoster, 2006.

Anderson, Ray. *The Shape of Practical Theology: Empowering Ministry With Theological Praxis*. Downer's Grove, IL: InterVarsity, 2001.

Arn, Charles. "A Response to Dr. Rainer," *Journal of the American Society for Church Growth*, Vol. 6, 1995.

Aune, David E. *The New Testament in Its Literary Environment*. Philadelphia: Westminster, 1989.

Avalos, Hector. *Health Care and the Rise of Christianity*. Peabody: Hendrickson, 1999.

Bartchy, S. Scott. "Who Should Be Called 'Father'? Paul of Tarsus between the Jesus Tradition and *Patria Potestas*." *The Social World of the New Testament*, Edited by Jerome H. Neyrey and Eric C. Steward. Peabody: Hendrickson, 2008.

Bellville, Linda L. "'Imitate Me, Just as I Imitate Christ': Discipleship in the Corinthian Correspondence," edited by Richard N. Longenecker, 120–42. *Patterns of Discipleship in the New Testament*. Grand Rapids: Eerdmans, 1996.

Biblia Hebraica Stuttgartensia. Edited by Karl Ellinger and Wilhelm Rudooph. Stuttgart: Deutsche Biblestiftung, 1977.

Boersma, Hans. *Violence, Hospitality, and the Cross: Reappropriating the Atonement Tradition*. Grand Rapids: Baker, 2004.

Bookidis, Nancy. "Religion in Corinth: 146 B.C.E. to 100 C.E. In *Urban Religion in Roman Corinth*, edited by Daniel N. Schowalter and Steven J. Friesen, 141–64. Cambridge: Harvard University, 2005.

Carlin, George. *When Will Jesus Bring the Pork Chops?* New York: Hyperion, 2004.

Chrysostom, John. *Proem NPNF*.

Cicero, *Duties*.

Clark, Gillian. *Christianity and Roman Society*. NY: Cambridge, 2004.

Clark, Ron. "Associating with the Humiliated: Using Victim's Testimonies to Teach Religion to College Students in an Academic Setting," *Journal of Religion and Abuse* 7:1 (May 2005).

———. *Emerging Elders: Developing Shepherds in God's Image*. Abilene, TX: Leafwood, 2008.

———. *Setting the Captives Free: A Christian Theology of Domestic Abuse*. Eugene, OR: Cascade, 2005.

Clarke, Andrew D. *First Century Christians in the Graeco-Roman World Serve the Community of the Christ: Christians as Leaders and Ministers*. Grand Rapids: Eerdmans, 2000.

———. *Secular and Christian Leadership in Corinth: A Socio-Historical and Exegetical Study of 1 Corinthians 1–6*, reprint. Paternoster: Great Britain 2006.

Bibliography

Clegg, Tom and Warren Bird. *Lost in America*. Loveland, CO: Group Publishing, 2001.
Clement of Alexandria. *The Stromata*.
Clement of Rome, *1 Clement*.
Davis, James A. *Wisdom and Spirit: An Investigation of 1 Corinthians 1.18–3.20 Against the Background of Jewish Sapiential Traditions in the Greco-Roman Period*. New York: University Press, 1984.
de Vos, Craig Steven. *Church and Community Conflict: The Relationships of the Thessalonian, Corinthian, and Philippian Churches with Their Wider Civic Communities*. Atlanta: Scholar's Press, 1999.
Dio Chrysostom, *Oratio*.
Engelbrecht, Edward A. "'To Speak in a Tongue': The Old Testament and Early Rabbinic Background of a Pauline Expression," *Concordia Journal 22 (1996)*.
Fant, Clyde E. and Mitchell G. Reddish, *A Guide to Biblical Sites in Greece and Turkey*. New York: Oxford, 2003.
Friesen, Steven J. "Prospects for a Demography of the Pauline Mission: Corinth Among the Churches." In *Urban Religion in Roman Corinth*, edited by Daniel N. Schowalter and Steven J. Friesen, 351–70. Cambridge: Harvard University, 2005.
Gebhard, Elizabeth R. "Rites for Melikertes-Palaimon in the Early Roman Corinthia." In *Urban Religion in Roman Corinth*, edited by Daniel N. Schowalter and Steven J. Friesen, 165–203. Cambridge: Harvard University, 2005.
Harland, Philip A. *Associations, Synagogues, and Congregations: Claiming a Place in Ancient Mediterranean Society*. Minneapolis: Fortress, 2003.
Hellerman, Joseph H. *The Ancient Church as Family*. Minneapolis: Fortress, 2001.
Howard, James M. *Paul the Community, and Progressive Sanctification: An Exploration into Community-Based Transformation within Pauline Theology*. NY: Peter Lang, 2007.
Instone-Brewer, David. *Divorce and Remarriage in the Bible: The Social and Literary Context*. Grand Rapids: Eerdmans, 2002.
Jeffers, James S. *The Greco-Roman World of the New Testament Era: Exploring the Background of Early Christianity*. Downer's Grove, IL: InterVarsity, 1999.
Judge, E. A. *Social Distinctives of the Christians in the First Century: Pivotal Essays By E. A. Judge*. Ed. David M. Scholer. Peabody: Hendrickson, 2008.
Justin Martyr. *2 Apology*.
Juvenal, *Satires*. Translated by Hubert Creekmore. NY: The New American Library, 1963.
King, Martin Luther, Jr. *Why We Can't Wait*. NY: Mentor, 1964.
Klauck, Hans-Josef. *The Religious Context of Early Christianity: A Guide to Graeco-Roman Religions*. Minneapolis: Fortress, 2003.
Kraemer, Ross Shephard. ed. *Women's Religions in the Greco-Roman World A Sourcebook*. New York: Oxford, 2004.
Lampe, Peter. "The Corinthian Eucharistic Dinner Party: Exegesis of a Cultural Context (1 Cor. 11:17–34)," *Affirmation* 4 (1991): 1–16.
Lanci, John R. "The Stones Don't Speak and the Texts Tell Lies: Sacred Sex at Corinth." In *Urban Religion in Roman Corinth*, edited by Daniel N. Schowalter and Steven J. Friesen, 205–20. Cambridge: Harvard University, 2005.
LaVey, Anton Szandor. *The Satanic Bible*. NY: Avon, 1969.
Lewis, Robert and Rob Wilkins, *The Church of Irresistible Influence*. Grand Rapids: Zondervan, 2001. LaVey, Anton Szandor. *The Satanic Bible*. NY: Avon, 1969.
Livy, *Ab Urbe Condita Libri*.
Loyd, Ken. *They're Gentiles for Christ's Sake*. Portland: Bridge-PDX Publishing, 2001.

Longenecker, Richard N. Ed. *Patterns of Discipleship in the New Testament*. Grand Rapids: Eerdmans, 1996.
Maccoby, Hyam. *The Myth Maker: Paul and the Invention of Christianity*. NY: Barnes and Noble, 1986.
McIntosh, Gary L. *Biblical Church Growth: How You Can Work with God to Build a Faithful Church*. Grand Rapids: Baker, 2003.
Nappo, Salvatore. *Pompeii: A Guide to the Ancient City*. NY: Barnes and Noble, 1998.
Nietzsche, Frederich. *The Anti-Christ*, trans. H. L. Mencken. Tucson: See Sharp, 1999.
———. *Beyond Good and Evil: A Prelude to a Philosophy of the Future*, trans. Walter Kaufmann. NY: Vintage, 1966.
Novum Testamentum Graeca, 27th ed. Edited by Eberhard Nestle, Erwin Nestle, Barbara Aland, Kurt Aland, Johannes Karavidopoulos, Carlo M. Martini, Bruce Metzger. Stuttgart: Deutsche Bibelgesellschaft, 1993.
O'Connor, Jerome Murphy. *1 Corinthians*. 2nd Ed. Collegeville: Liturgical, 1991.
———. *St. Paul's Corinth: Texts and Archaeology*. Collegeville, MN: Liturgical Press, 1983.
Osiek, Carolyn and David L. Bach, *Families in the New Testament World*. Louisville: Westminster/John Knox, 1997.
Oster, Rick. *1 Corinthians*. Joplin: College Press, 1995.
———. "When Men Wore Veils to Worship: Historical Context of I Cor. 11:4," *New Testament Studies* 34 (1988): 481–505.
Paige, Terence. "Stoicism, ἐλευθερία and Community at Corinth,"207–18. *Christianity at Corinth: The Quest for the Pauline Church*. Ed. Edward Adams and David G. Horrell. Louisville: Westminster John/Knox, 2004.
Pausanias, *Decription of Greece.*
Theophilus. *To Autolycus.*
Thom Rainer, *Kairos Church Planting Summit*, September 2005, St. Louis, MO.
———. *The Unchurched Next Door*. Grand Rapids: Zondervan, 2003.
Richards, E. Randolph. *Paul and First-Century Letter Writing: Secretaries, Composition and Collection*. Downer's Grove: InterVarsity Press, 2004.
Robinson, Betsey A. "Fountains and the Formation of Cultural Identity at Roman Corinth. In *Urban Religion in Roman Corinth*, edited by Daniel N. Schowalter and Steven J. Friesen, 111–140. Cambridge: Harvard University, 2005.
Rufus, Musonius. Trans. by Cora E. Lutz, "Musonius Rufus: 'The Roman Socrates,'" *Yale Classical Studies* 10 (1947).
Scanlon, Thomas F. *Eros and Greek Athletics*. New York: Oxford, 2002.
Sigountos, James G. "The Genre of 1 Corinthians 13," *N T S* 40 (1994): 246–60.
deSilva, David A. "'Let the One Who Claims Honor Establish That Claim in the Lord': Honor Discourse in the Corinthian Correspondence." *BTB* 28:2 (Summer 1998): 61–74.
Smit, J. F. M. "Two Puzzles: 1 Corinthians 12.31 and 13.3 A Rhetorical Solution," *NTS* 39 (1993): 246–64.
Smith, Dennis E. *From Symposium To Eucharist: The Banquet in the Early Christian World*. Minneapolis: Fortress, 2003.
Stetzer, Ed and Philip Connor. *Research Report: Church Plant Survivability and Health Study 2007*. Center For Missional Research, North American Mission Board, 2007.
Strabo, *Geography.*

Theissen, Gerd. *The Social Setting of Pauline Christianity: Essays on Corinth*. Philadelphia: Fortress, 1982.
Tripolitis, Antonia. *Religions of the Hellenistic-Roman Age*. Grand Rapids: Eerdmans, 2002.
Walbank, Mary E. Hoskins. "Unquiet Graves: Burial Practices of the Roman Corinthians." In *Urban Religion in Roman Corinth*, edited by Daniel N. Schowalter and Steven J. Friesen, 249–80. Cambridge: Harvard University, 2005.
Wallace-Hadrill, Andrew. *Houses and Society in Pompeii and Herculaneum*. Princeton, NJ: Princeton University, 1994.
Walters, James. "Civic Identity in Roman Corinth and Its Impact on Early Churches." In *Urban Religion in Roman Corinth*, edited by Daniel N. Schowalter and Steven J. Friesen, 397–417. Cambridge: Harvard University, 2005.
Ward, Roy Bown. "Musonius and Paul on Marriage," *New Testament Studies* 36 (1990): 281–89.
Welborn, Laurence L. "Discord in Corinth: first Corinthians 1–4 and Ancient Politics." 139–44. *Christianity at Corinth: The Quest for the Pauline Church*. Ed. Edward Adams and David G. Horrell. Louisville: Westminster John/Knox, 2004.
White, Joel R. "'Baptized On Account of the Dead': The Meaning of 1 Corinthians 15:29 in its Context," *Journal of Biblical Literature* 116:3 (1997): 487–99.
Williams, Charles K. III. "Roman Corinth: The Final Years of Pagan Cult Facilities Along East Theater Street." In *Urban Religion in Roman Corinth*, edited by Daniel N. Schowalter and Steven J. Friesen, 221–47. Cambridge: Harvard University, 2005.
Winter, Bruce W. *After Paul Left Corinth: The Influence of Secular Ethics and Social Change*. Grand Rapids: Eerdmans, 2001.
———. *Roman Wives, Roman Widows: The Appearance of New Women and the Pauline Communities*. Grand Rapids: Eerdmans, 2003.
Witherington, Ben III. *Conflict and Community in Corinth: A Socio-Rhetorical Commentary on 1 and 2 Corinthians*. Grand Rapids, MI: Eerdmans, 1995.
Xenophon, *Memor*.

www.ingramcontent.com/pod-product-compliance
Lightning Source LLC
Chambersburg PA
CBHW071229170426
43191CB00032B/1209